MICROCONTROLLER APPLICATIONS

AUTHOR

Dr. Ritula Thakur

Associate Professor,
National Institute of Technical Teachers Training & Research,
Chandigarh

REVIEWER

Dr. Philip Cherian

Associate Professor, College of Engineering,
Kallooppara

KHANNA BOOK PUBLISHING CO. (P) Ltd.
4C/4344, Ansari Road, Darya Ganj,
New Delhi, India

All India Council for Technical Education
Nelson Mandela Marg, Vasant Kunj,
New Delhi, India

Dear Readers,

To prevent the piracy, this book is secured with HIGH SECURITY HOLOGRAM on the front title cover. In case you don't find the hologram on the front cover title, please write us to at contact@khannabooks.com or whatsapp us at +91-99109 09320 and avail special gift voucher for yourself.

Specimen of Hologram on front Cover title:

Moreover, there is a SPECIAL DISCOUNT COUPON for you with EVERY HOLOGRAM.

How to avail this SPECIAL DISCOUNT:
Step 1: Scratch the hologram
Step 2: Under the scratch area, your "coupon code" is available
Step 3: Logon to www.khannabooks.com
Step 4: Use your "coupon code" in the shopping cart and get your copy at a special discount
Step 5: Enjoy your reading!

ISBN: 978-93-5538-504-8
Book Code: DIP500EN

Microcontroller Applications
by Dr. Ritula Thakur

First Edition: 2026

Originally Published by:
All India Council for Technical Education, Ministry of Education, GOI

Exclusively Published & Distributed by:
Khanna Book Publishing Co. (P) Ltd.
4C/4344, Ansari Road, Daryaganj,
New Delhi (INDIA)

Visit us at: **www.khannabooks.com**
Write us at: **contact@khannabooks.com**

To view complete list of books, Please scan the QR Code: KPH

Printed in Bharat.

प्रो. टी. जी. सीताराम
अध्यक्ष
Prof. T. G. Sitharam
Chairman

सत्यमेव जयते

आज़ादी का अमृत महोत्सव

अखिल भारतीय तकनीकी शिक्षा परिषद्
(भारत सरकार का एक सांविधिक निकाय)
(शिक्षा मंत्रालय, भारत सरकार)
नेल्सन मंडेला मार्ग, वसंत कुंज, नई दिल्ली–110070
दूरभाष : 011–26131498
ई–मेल : chairman@aicte-india.org

ALL INDIA COUNCIL FOR TECHNICAL EDUCATION
(A STATUTORY BODY OF THE GOVT. OF INDIA)
(Ministry of Education, Govt. of India)
Nelson Mandela Marg, Vasant Kunj, New Delhi-110070
Phone : 011-26131498
E-mail : chairman@aicte-india.org

FOREWORD

Engineers are the backbone of any modern society. They are the ones responsible for the marvels as well as the improved quality of life across the world. Engineers have driven humanity towards greater heights in a more evolved and unprecedented manner.

The All India Council for Technical Education (AICTE), have spared no efforts towards the strengthening of the technical education in the country. AICTE is always committed towards promoting quality Technical Education to make India a modern developed nation emphasizing on the overall welfare of mankind.

An array of initiatives has been taken by AICTE in last decade which have been accelerated now by the National Education Policy (NEP) 2020. The implementation of NEP under the visionary leadership of Hon'ble Prime Minister of India envisages the provision for education in regional languages to all, thereby ensuring that every graduate becomes competent enough and is in a position to contribute towards the national growth and development through innovation & entrepreneurship.

One of the spheres where AICTE had been relentlessly working since past couple of years is providing high quality original technical contents at Under Graduate & Diploma level prepared and translated by eminent educators in various Indian languages to its aspirants. For students pursuing 2nd year of their Engineering education, AICTE has identified 87 books, which shall be translated into 12 Indian languages - Hindi, Tamil, Gujarati, Odia, Bengali, Kannada, Urdu, Punjabi, Telugu, Marathi, Assamese & Malayalam. In addition to the English medium, books in different Indian Languages are going to support the students to understand the concepts in their respective mother tongue.

On behalf of AICTE, I express sincere gratitude to all distinguished authors, reviewers and translators from the renowned institutions of high repute for their admirable contribution in a record span of time.

AICTE is confident that these outcomes based original contents shall help aspirants to master the subject with comprehension and greater ease.

(Prof. T. G. Sitharam)

ACKNOWLEDGEMENT

Writing a book on microcontrollers has been a challenging yet rewarding journey, and it would not have been possible without the support and guidance of several individuals and organizations.

I am grateful to the authorities of AICTE, particularly Prof. (Dr.) T G Sitharam, Chairman; Dr. Abhay Jere, Vice-Chairman, Prof. Rajive Kumar, Member-Secretary, Dr. Sunil Luthra, and Reena Sharma, Hindi Officer Training and Learning Bureau for their planning to publish this book on Microcontroller Applications. I sincerely acknowledge the valuable contributions of the reviewer of the book Dr. Philip Cherian, Associate Professor, College of Engineering, Kallooppara, Kerala.

I am also thankful to director of my institute, Prof. Bhola Ram Gurja, whose vision and guidance are truly invaluable to us. I am also thankful to my Head of department, Prof. Lini Mathew, whose unwavering support has always motivated me to try new initiatives. I am also thankful to my department, particularly, Ms. Divya Sharma, who helped me time and again in bringing this book to this final shape.

I would also like to acknowledge the contributions of the open-source community and the developers of various microcontroller tools and libraries that were essential for the practical aspects of this book. Your work continues to inspire innovation and learning.

To my family and friends, particularly my husband Dr. Babankumar and son Vihaan, thank you for your patience, love, and understanding during the many hours I spent working on this book. Your constant support gave me the strength to see this project through to the end.

This book is the culmination of many efforts, and I am grateful to everyone who played a part in making it a reality.

Dr. Ritula Thakur

PREFACE

Drawing from extensive classroom teaching experience, this textbook on "Microcontroller Applications" is designed to give students a strong understanding of the subject. Written in clear and straightforward language, it guides readers through the key technical concepts of microcontrollers, focusing on the everyday use of Embedded Systems in daily life and workplaces. This book is ideal for a one-semester course for diploma students in Electrical, Electronics and Communication Engineering, Electrical and Electronics Engineering, and Electronics & Instrumentation Engineering.

This book is organised in total 6 units. The outline of the book is as follows:

First unit describes an exploration of the evolution of microcontrollers, tracing their development from their inception to the present day. The fundamental concepts are then explored by discussing the block diagram of a microcomputer, highlighting its key elements and functionalities. Furthermore, differences between Von Neumann and Harvard architectures are examined, discussing their unique characteristics and applications. Lastly, the significance of microcontrollers is addressed by explaining the specific needs they fulfill in modern technology, underscoring their versatility and importance in embedded systems and beyond

Second unit delves into the intricate architecture of the 8051 microcontroller, understanding its key components and fundamental organization. The memory structure of the 8051 is explored, comprehensively covering both ROM and RAM, thus gaining insight into how data is stored and accessed within these memory spaces. With a thorough grasp of the Pin Diagram, we can learn to design and execute basic applications leveraging the capabilities of the 8051 microcontroller effectively. Additionally, we developed the ability to discern between general-purpose registers, special function registers, and program status registers, through which we can enhance our proficiency in programming and utilize the 8051 microcontroller to its fullest potential.

Third unit of this book delves into the instruction set of the 8051 microcontroller, understanding various addressing modes. The readers will gain insight into how instructions are classified. With a thorough understanding of the instruction set, we can learn to write programs for 8051 microcontroller effectively. Through this chapter, we have laid a solid foundation in assembly language programming of the 8051 microcontroller, equipping ourselves with essential knowledge and skills to embark on more advanced projects and applications.

The fourth unit deals with Embedded C programming for the 8051 microcontroller, dealing with essential aspects crucial for programming within this embedded system. The syntax specific to Embedded C for the 8051 is examined, highlighting its nuances and conventions for effective programming. Through these discussions, readers can gain a comprehensive understanding of how to leverage Embedded C to develop robust and efficient solutions for the 8051 microcontroller.

The fifth unit covers essential features of the 8051 microcontroller, focusing on its timers and counters, serial communication, interrupts, and power-saving operations. First subsection explains the configuration and usage of the 8051's timers and counters, highlighting their role in timing operations and event counting. Serial communication explains the usage of the 8051's timers and counters, highlighting their role in timing operations and event counting. Then the unit introduces the concept of interrupts, explaining how the 8051 handles external and internal events efficiently. Finally, the unit discusses various power-saving modes available in the 8051, such as idle and power-down modes, which are crucial for energy-efficient designs.

The sixth unit on Software Development tools for the 8051 microcontroller deals with essential aspects crucial for programming for developing embedded systems. It starts by exploring various software development tools utilized in development of 8051 programming. Subsequently, it explains in detail the Keil compilers required for creating Hex files from assembly language and Embedded C programs. Lastly, practical development of the project is examined by burning the created hex file into the microcontroller using Flash magic software. Through these discussions, readers gained a comprehensive understanding of how to develop robust and efficient solutions for the 8051 microcontroller.

Dr. Ritula Thakur

OUTCOME BASED EDUCATION

For the implementation of an outcome based education the first requirement is to develop an outcome based curriculum and incorporate an outcome based assessment in the education system. By going through outcome based assessments evaluators will be able to evaluate whether the students have achieved the outlined standard, specific and measurable outcomes. With the proper incorporation of outcome based education there will be a definite commitment to achieve a minimum standard for all learners without giving up at any level. At the end of the programme running with the aid of outcome based education, a student will be able to arrive at the following outcomes:

PO1. Basic and Discipline specific knowledge: Apply knowledge of basic mathematics, science and engineering fundamentals and engineering specialization to solve the engineering problems.

PO2. Problem analysis: Identify and analyses well-defined engineering problems using codified standard methods.

PO3. Design/development of solutions: Design solutions for well-defined technical problems and assist with the design of systems components or processes to meet specified needs.

PO4. Engineering Tools, Experimentation and Testing: Apply modern engineering tools and appropriate technique to conduct standard tests and measurements.

PO5. Engineering practices for society, sustainability and environment: Apply appropriate technology in context of society, sustainability, environment and ethical practices.

PO6. Project Management: Use engineering management principles individually, as a team member or a leader to manage projects and effectively communicate about well-defined engineering activities.

PO7. Life-long learning: Ability to analyse individual needs and engage in updating in the context of technological changes.

COURSE OUTCOMES

After completion of the course, the students will be able to:

CO1- Interpret the salient features of various types of microcontrollers

CO2- Interpret the salient features of archetype of types microcontrollers IC 8051

CO3- Maintain the program features of the Microcontroller based application

CO4- Develop assembly language program

CO5- Develop programs to interface 8051 microcontrollers with LED/SWITCH

Mapping of Course Outcomes with Programme Outcomes to be done according to the matrix given below:

Course Outcomes	Expected Mapping with Programme Outcomes *(1- Weak Correlation; 2- Medium correlation; 3- Strong Correlation)*						
	PO-1	**PO-2**	**PO-3**	**PO-4**	**PO-5**	**PO-6**	**PO-7**
CO-1	3	2	2	1	2	1	3
CO-2	3	3	3	3	2	2	3
CO-3	3	3	2	3	2	2	3
CO-4	3	3	2	2	1	2	1
CO-5	3	2	1	2	1	1	2

GUIDELINES FOR TEACHERS

To implement Outcome Based Education (OBE) the knowledge level and skill set of the students should be enhanced. Teachers should take a major responsibility for the proper implementation of OBE. Some of the responsibilities (not limited to) for the teachers in OBE system may be as follows:

- Within reasonable constraints, they should manipulate time to the best advantage of all students.
- They should assess the students only upon certain defined criterion without considering any other potential ineligibility to discriminate them.
- They should try to grow the learning abilities of the students to a certain level before they leave the institute.
- They should try to ensure that all the students are equipped with quality knowledge as well as competence after they finish their education.
- They should always encourage the students to develop their ultimate performance capabilities.
- They should facilitate and encourage group work and team work to consolidate newer approach.
- They should follow Blooms taxonomy in every part of the assessment.

Bloom's Taxonomy

Level	Teacher should Check	Student should be able to	Possible Mode of Assessment
Create	Students ability to create	Design or Create	Mini project
Evaluate	Students ability to justify	Argue or Defend	Assignment
Analyse	Students ability to distinguish	Differentiate or Distinguish	Project/Lab Methodology
Apply	Students ability to use information	Operate or Demonstrate	Technical Presentation/ Demonstration
Understand	Students ability to explain the ideas	Explain or Classify	Presentation/Seminar
Remember	Students ability to recall (or remember)	Define or Recall	Quiz

GUIDELINES FOR STUDENTS

Students should take equal responsibility for implementing the OBE. Some of the responsibilities (not limited to) for the students in OBE system are as follows:

- Students should be well aware of each UO before the start of a unit in each and every course.
- Students should be well aware of each CO before the start of the course.
- Students should be well aware of each PO before the start of the programme.
- Students should think critically and reasonably with proper reflection and action.
- Learning of the students should be connected and integrated with practical and real life consequences.
- Students should be well aware of their competency at every level of OBE.

LIST OF ABBREVIATIONS

Abbreviations	Full Form
PPI	Programmable Peripheral Interface
CPU	Central Processing Unit
RAM	Random Access Memory
ROM	Read Only Memory
IDEs	Integrated development Environments
IoT	Internet of Things
ALU	Arithmetic Logic Unit
GPU	Graphic Processing Unit
T0,T1	Timers
INT0,INT1	Interrupts
DPTR	Data Pointer
PSW	Program Status Word
CY	Carry
AC	Auxiliary Carry/Auxiliary Flag
O	Overflow
P	Parity
A	Accumulator
BCD	Binary Coded Decimal
PC	Program Counter
DPH	Data Pointer High
DPL	Data Pointer Low
SFR	Special Function Register
EA	External Access
SP	Stack Pointer
TMRx	Timer/Counter Registers
SCON	Serial Port Control
SBUF	Serial Port Data Buffer
IE	Interrupt Enable
IP	Interrupt Priority
DIP	Dual in line Package
LLC	Leadless Chip Carrier
QFP	Quad Flat Package
WR	Write
RD	Read
PSEN	Program Store Enable
OE	Output Enable
ALE	Address Latch Enable

Abbreviations	Full Form
OV	Overflow
RET	Return
LJMP	Long Jump
SJMP	Short Jump
LSB	Least Significant Bit
MSB	Most Significant Bit
ISR	Interrupt Service Routine
EI	Enable Interrupts
DI	Disable Interrupts
ORG	Origin
DB	Define Byte
DW	Define Word
EQU	Equate
MOV	Move
TL0	Timer 0 Low Byte
TH0	Timer 0 High Byte
TL1	Timer 1 Low Byte
TH1	Timer 1 High Byte
TMOD	Timer Mode
TR	Timer Start
TF	Timer Flag
SPI	Special Peripheral Interface
I2C	Inter-Integrated Circuit
UART	Universal Asynchronous Receiver/Transmitter
USART	Universal Synchronous Asynchronous Receiver/Transmitter
RI	Receive Interrupt
TI	Transmit Interrupt
ISP	In System Programming

LIST OF FIGURES

Unit 1

Unit 2

Unit 3

Unit 5

Unit 6

CONTENTS

1 Introduction to Microcontrollers

UNIT SPECIFICS

This unit elaborately discusses the following topics:

- Evolution of Microcontrollers
- Block Diagram of Microcomputer
- Elements of Microcomputer
- Types of Buses
- Von Neuman and Harvard Architecture
- Comparison of Microprocessor and Micrcocontroller
- Need of Microcontroller
- Family of Microcontrollers and their Specifications
- Versions of Microcontroller 8951

The questions at the back of chapter are mainly a large number of multiple choice questions as well as questions of short and long answer types. In order to inspire a deeper understanding among students, both lower and higher order of Bloom's taxonomy have been used to frame the questions. Further, a list of references and suggested readings are given in the unit. Some QR codes have also been provided in different sections which can be scanned for relevant supportive knowledge.

RATIONALE

This basic unit on introduction to microcontrollers introduces the students to the world of embedded systems and role of microcontrollers in shaping our life.

PRE-REQUISITES

Knowledge of digital systems and basics of microprocessors

UNIT OUTCOMES

After completing the unit, the students will be able to:

U1-O1: Discuss the evolution of microcontrollers

U1-O2: Explain the block diagram of a microcomputer and its elements

U1-O3: Differentiate between Von Neuman and Harvard Architecture

U1-O4: Compare a microprocessor with a microcontroller

U1-O5: Explain the need for a microcontroller

Unit-1 Outcomes	EXPECTED MAPPING WITH COURSE OUTCOMES (*1- Weak Correlation; 2- Medium correlation; 3- Strong Correlation*)					
	CO-1	CO-2	CO-3	CO-4	CO-5	CO-6
U1-O1	3	2	3	2	1	3
U1-O2	1	2	3	2	3	1
U1-O3	3	3	2	2	2	3
U1-O4	2	2	1	2	3	2
U1-O5	2	2	2	2	3	2

1.1 Evolution of Microcontrollers

Microcontrollers, small computing devices with a decades-long history, are often overlooked but have significantly impacted industries like automotive and consumer electronics. Serving as the central processing units in embedded systems, they play a crucial role in advancing technology and can be found in everyday devices, from washing machines to advanced medical equipment.

The following sections cover various significant milestones in the evolution of microcontrollers, highlighting the key developments that greatly influenced this technology.

1.1.1 The Early Days

Microcontrollers originated in the 1960s to meet the demand for compact computing solutions. Intel, a major player founded in 1968, played a crucial role. In 1971, Intel introduced the 4004 microprocessor, often regarded as the precursor to microcontrollers. With 2300 transistors, the 4004 was a pioneering 4-bit processor initially designed for calculators. Although not as advanced as today's microcontrollers, it marked the beginning of integrating computing capabilities onto a single chip. However, a microprocessor does not contain RAM, ROM, I/O ports, Timer/Counters, Serial Ports, interrupts and are commonly known as general-purpose microprocessors. For example, in order to connect a microprocessor with the real world, Input/Output ports are required. Since a microprocessor does not have on chip I/O ports of its own, an external chip known as 8255- Programmable Peripheral Interface (PPI) needs to be interfaced with it.In order to make it a complete functional unit, all these peripherals are to be externally attached to a microprocessor. This makes the microprocessor based system costly as well as bulky. The need for compact, self-contained computing units led to the development of early microcontrollers in the mid-1970s.

1.1.2 The Birth of Microcontrollers

The true journey of microcontrollers started with Intel 8048 in 1976. This 8-bit microcontroller combined a central processing unit (CPU), random-access memory (RAM), read-only memory (ROM), and input/output (I/O) peripherals on a single chip, making it a self-contained computing device. The fixed amount of on-chip memory (ROM, RAM) and I/O ports in microcontroller led to its widespread use across diverse applications where cost and space are crucial, ranging from automotive control systems to consumer electronics. Shortly after, big semiconductor companies like Motorola and Texas Instruments entered the scene, speeding up the progress of microcontrollers.

1.1.3 The 8-Bit Revolution

The 1980s witnessed the 8-bit microcontroller revolution. Manufacturers like Intel, Microchip, Atmel and Zilog emerged as major players, introducing powerful and cost-effective 8-bit microcontrollers with enhanced capabilities, such as improved memory, increased processing speed, and additional peripherals. The introduction of Flash memory in microcontrollers around this time revolutionized the industry, allowing for reprogrammability expanding their applications across diverse industries.

1.1.4 The Rise of 16-Bit and 32-Bit Microcontrollers

In the 1990s, the semiconductor industry evolved tremendously with shrinking transistor size and more efficient manufacturing of ICs. This enabled the integration of larger memory banks and increased computational capabilities within a single chip.

At the same time, applications such as real-time processing, intricate data manipulation, and sophisticated control systems demanded higher computing capabilities, the limitations of 8-bit microcontrollers became evident. Thus came 16-bit and 32-bit microcontrollers into picture offering higher performance, improved capabilities and more extensive memory and literally revolutionized the scenario of embedded systems, thus setting the stage for unprecedented technological advancements.

The rising popularity of 16-bit and 32-bit microcontrollers was also influenced by advancements in software development tools. The availability of user-friendly integrated development environments (IDEs), compilers, and debugging tools facilitated the creation of complex software applications for these microcontrollers. This synergy between hardware and software development ecosystems played a crucial role in accelerating the extensive acceptance of 16-bit and 32-bit microcontrollers.

ARM, a prominent semiconductor company based in the United Kingdom, became a major player in this domain, providing energy-efficient and high-performance processor cores that found extensive adoption among various manufacturers.

1.1.5 Contemporary Landscape

Today, microcontrollers play a crucial role in driving the Internet of Things (IoT) revolution. The demand for intelligent features and good connectivity has led to the incorporation of sophisticated peripherals and wireless communication modules into microcontrollers. This has fueled the development of technologies such as smart homes, wearable devices, and industrial automation.

In a nutshell, it can be said that the evolution of microcontrollers is a testament to the continual quest for enhanced performance, integration as well as miniaturization in the field of computing. Starting from modest 4004 microprocessor and advancing to the sophisticated 32-bit microcontrollers propelling today's cutting-edge technologies, this evolution has significantly altered the landscape of embedded systems. Moving forward, the continued innovation in microcontroller technology promises even greater possibilities, propelling progress across diverse industries and influencing the future of interconnected devices.

SCAN HERE (To Know more details about history of 8051)

1.2 Block Diagram of Microcomputer

A microcomputer is a computer whose most important components are integrated in an IC chip which is referred to as the microprocessor. Today, PCs are miniaturized and low cost personal computers have come to dominate many aspects of modern life. There have been remarkable developments in microcomputing since their introduction into the market, including many improvements to processing power, memory capacity and also connectivity. They serve many different purposes including personal productivity, gameplay, content generation and scientific progress as well as business. Portability and affordability of the microcomputers have certainly played a very important role in democratizing computing power worldwide, becoming a part of our everyday life. The block diagram of a microcontroller is shown in Fig.1.1.

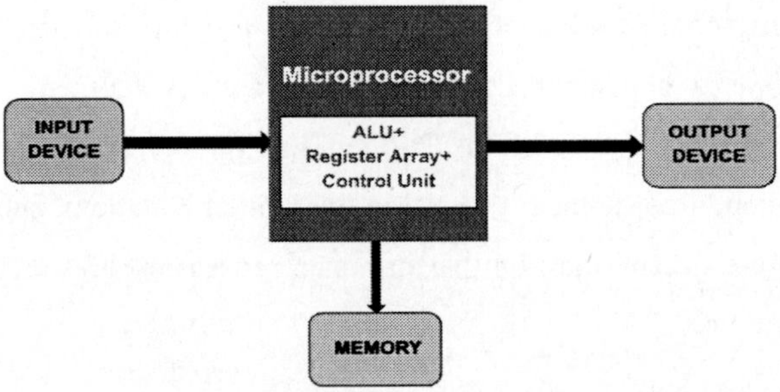

Fig. 1.1 Block Diagram of a Microcomputer

1.3 Elements of Microcomputer

A microcomputer has important parts that make it work. The main part is the central processing unit (CPU), which does calculations and follows instructions. Memory has RAM for temporary storage and ROM for permanent storage. Input devices like keyboards and mouse give information to the microcomputer, while output devices like monitors and printers show the processed information. Storage devices, such as hard drives, keep data for a long time. The system bus helps different parts communicate, and the motherboard connects everything together. These parts work together to make the microcomputer do tasks, store data, and interact with users in various ways.

The key components of a microcomputer are discussed in the subsequent subsections:

1.3.1 Microprocessor

The CPU is the brain of the microcomputer, which implements commands and also does calculations. It is a one-chip integrated circuit with an ALU, control unit and also registers.

Memory: There are two forms of memory found in the microcomputers: volatile and also non-volatile. Volatile memory like RAM (Random Access Memory) is used for the temporary storage of data and program code while non-volatile memory such as ROM (Read Only Memory) is for storing firmware instructions that do not change under regular usage.

1.3.2 Storage

Permanent storage is performed by the microcomputers using HDDs, SSD or external storages. These gadgets allow the users to store and recover information despite the computer supply of electricity being cut off.

1.3.3 Input Devices

Keyboards, mice and also touchscreens are some of the devices that help users to input the data into microcomputer. These input devices are the very essential tools for communicating with the software programs and also controlling operating systems.

1.3.4 Output Devices

Monitors, printers and speakers on the part of microcomputers are used as output devices. These gadgets show information in present the hard copies of documents and also allow users to see what has resulted from their interactions with the computer.

1.3.5 Motherboard

The motherboard is the central circuit board that provides a link and communication between the different parts of a microcomputer. It accommodates the CPU, memory modules and also connectors of peripherals.

1.3.6 Peripheral Devices

Microcomputers can be extended with many peripheral devices such as printers, scanners, external storage and also networking. Such peripherals complement the microcomputer and are also designed to meet specific user requirements.

1.4 Types of Buses

One of the essential components within a microcontroller architecture is the bus system. The transportation of communication and data transfer amongst distinct modules inside the microcontroller is made possible with the help of buses; hence, coordination between various parts becomes better. There are mainly three types of buses in a microcontroller namely - (i) Address Bus (ii) Data Bus and (iii) Control Bus as given in Fig. 1.2.

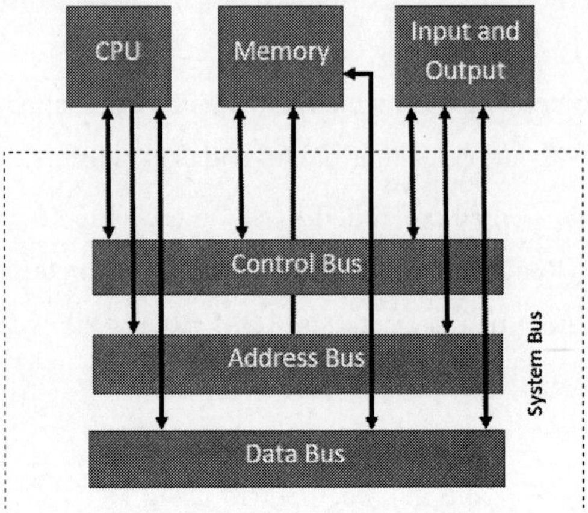

Fig.1.2 Different Buses in a Microcontroller

The role as well as important information concerning these buses are discussed in following subsections.

1.4.1 Address Bus

The address bus is a critical component of a microcontroller's bus system, responsible for transmitting the memory address from the central processing unit (CPU) to the memory modules. It determines the location in the memory where data is to be read from or written to. It specifies the particular memory location from which data is to be read or to where it has to be stored. The size of the address bus decides how much memory a microcontroller can use.

1.4.2 Data Bus

Data bus is another prime element of the connectivity system in microcontrollers, allowing data to be transferred in both directions between the CPU and other peripheral devices. The data bus width determines the number of bits that a system can pass during a single clock cycle. A data bus can be a parallel or serial bus depending on how the data is carried. A parallel bus is used in case of complex connections, which require more than one bit simultaneously. Serial buses send the data and receive data using only one wire, which is very simple when compared with parallel bus connections.

1.4.3 Control Bus

The control bus is a bidirectional bus that carries control signals between the microcontroller and other parts such as Input/Output devices and memory. It handles various control signals that coordinate and control the operations within the microcontroller such as read and write operations, interrupts, and clock synchronization. It ensures that different components of the microcontroller follow a synchronized sequence of operations and work in harmony.

1.5 Von Neuman and Harvard Architecture

As discussed earlier, a microprocessor-based system needs external components such as memory, I/O ports and timers to make a digital system. A microcontroller is a single-chip solution having all these components embedded inside a chip itself. Depending upon the memory bank for storing data and program, a microcontroller can have two types of architectures- Harvard Architecture and Von Neuman Architecture.

1.5.1 Von Neuman Architecture

The von Neumann architecture, also known as Princeton architecture, was initially proposed by John von Neumann an Hungarian–American mathematician and scientist in 1945. In this architecture, all electronics parts such as processing units, memory, as well as input-output devices, are connected by the means of one single system bus.

Structure of Von Neumann Architecture

The Von Neumann Architecture consists mainly of five key components: (i) Central Processing Unit (CPU), (ii)Memory, (iii) Input/Output (I/O) devices, (iv) Control Unit, and (v) Arithmetic and Logic Unit (ALU) as shown in Fig.1.3.

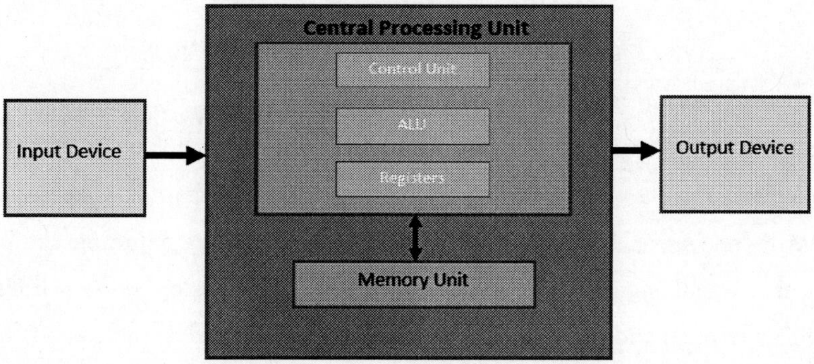

Fig.1.3 Structure of Von Neumann Architecture

The CPU acts as the brain of the system, helping in the execution of instructions and managing data processing. Memory stores both the data being processed and the instructions needed to perform tasks and is divided into two categories - data and program storage. The I/O devices enable communication with the external environment, the Control Unit oversees the execution of instructions, ensuring they are carried out in the correct sequence while the ALU handles arithmetic and logical operations of the system.

Advantages and Limitations of Von Neumann Architecture

Von Neumann Architecture offers several advantages, such as simplicity in design, ease of programming, and versatility. The stored program concept allows for the creation of complex programs and facilitates the development of high-level programming languages. However, the architecture is not without its limitations.

The sequential execution model can lead to bottlenecks in performance, and the shared bus system may result in data transfer delays.

1.5.2 Harvard Architecture

The Harvard architecture is a computer architecture design in which there are separate memories for data and instructions, which allows simultaneous access to both instruction and data. In this architecture, there are distinct and independent memory units for data and instructions, and they have separate buses for data and instructions. This separation of data and instruction memory is in contrast to the Von Neumann architecture, where a single memory space is used for both data and instructions. In Von Neumann architecture, data and instructions are fetched from the same memory pool using a unified bus.

The structure of Harvard architecture is shown in Fig. 1.4.

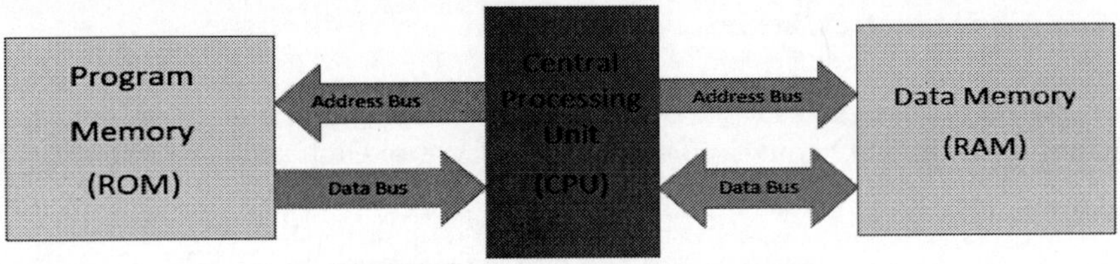

Fig.1.4 Structure of Harvard Architecture

Advantages and Limitations of Harvard Architecture

In Harvard architecture, the separation of data and instruction memory enhances the efficiency as well as overall processing speed and enables parallelism in instruction fetch and data access, as opposed to the sequential access found in von Neumann architecture. In applications requiring computing, such as in embedded systems, digital signal processing, and graphics processing units (GPUs) high, Harvard architecture's ability to fetch and process data concurrently contributes to reduced latency and improved overall system performance.

While Harvard architecture offers advantages such as simultaneous access to instructions and data, it does come with challenges, particularly in terms of programming complexity and memory management. The separation of instruction and data memories can require more careful handling by programmers, as they need to ensure that instructions and data are properly managed and that the correct memory spaces are accessed.

However, modern compilers and development tools are now available to mitigate these challenges. These tools can automate tasks related to managing separate instruction and data memories, making Harvard architecture more accessible for a broader range of applications.

1.6 Comparison between Microprocessor and Microcontrollers

In order to understand the differences between microprocessors and microcontrollers, it is very important to understand the basic working of a Central Processing Unit (CPU) of a computer. A CPU is basically the brain of a computer, it fetches, interprets, processes and executes the instructions and gives the output to do the work assigned to it. However, if we want to make a standalone application in a field, it is not possible to take the CPU everywhere. So with the advent of ICs and large scale integration of devices, it was possible to fabricate the functionalities of a CPU on a single chip itself, which came to be known as a microprocessor. Thus, in a layman's language, a microprocessor is known as "CPU on a chip". A microprocessor is a programmable device, which takes data from input devices such as mouse, keyboard etc, processes the data according to the instructions stored in the memory and sends the results either to some output device or stores it in memory. However, a microprocessor in itself cannot perform the digital operations alone because it does not contain any memory (RAM/ROM), Input/Output ports and are thus commonly known as general-purpose microprocessors. In order to make a complete functional unit, the system designer must add RAM, ROM, Input/Output ports, timers, Serial COM port externally to a microprocessor. The external addition of these peripherals makes the microprocessor based system bulkier and much more expensive.

As the technology of miniaturization of ICs advanced, the system designers came up with the idea of adding CPU (a microprocessor), memory (RAM/ROM), Input/Output ports, timers, Serial COM port on a single chip itself, which came to be known as a microcontroller. It was comparatively much cheaper in cost and compact as compared to microprocessor. The circuit design was also much simpler as external connections were comparatively reduced. The advent of microcontrollers completely took the industry by storm and became very popular in a very short time. While a microprocessor was known as "CPU on a chip" the microcontroller came to be known as "Computer on a chip". Although both microprocessor as well as microcontroller are IC devices and are primarily used in automating the process, there are striking differences between them. Microcontrollers are comparatively cheaper, compact and much simpler in design as compared to microprocessor based systems. The flexibility of adding external memory, input/output ports and timers to a microprocessor give the system designer versatility to decide on the amount of memory and I/O ports needed for a particular task. However, a microcontroller has fixed on-chip memory, timers as well as I/O ports, thus leaving little scope for the system designer to add them externally. Thus, a microprocessor is preferred for those applications which are general-purpose in nature, while a microcontroller being compact and lesser in cost is ideal for dedicated applications, in which cost and space are critical. Table 1.1 highlights the main differences between a microprocessor and a microcontroller.

(Scan to see video on Introduction to Microcontrollers)

Table 1.1 Differences between Microprocessor and Microcontroller

S. No.	Microprocessor	Microcontroller
1.	CPU on a chip	Computer on a chip
2.	It does not contain RAM, ROM, Input/Output ports, timers, Serial COM port	RAM, ROM, Input/Output ports, timers, Serial COM port are embedded on the chip itself
3.	Bulkier	Compact
4.	Costly	Cheaper
5.	Complex design	Simple design
6.	Flexibility to add external memory, I/O ports externally	No Versatility as on-chip memory, I/O ports are fixed
7.	Preferred for general-purpose applications	Preferred for dedicated applications

1.7 Need for a Microcontroller

As the world is becoming increasingly interconnected, the need for efficient and intelligent control systems has become very important. This is where the microcontrollers play a pivotal role in enhancing the way our daily devices function. As stated earlier, microcontroller being compact and lesser in cost is ideal for dedicated applications, in which cost and space are critical.

A microcontroller, a tiny but powerful integrated circuit, is found in an array of everyday gadgets, from washing machines and microwave ovens to cars and even wearable devices. One of the primary reasons for the widespread use of microcontrollers is their ability to process information and execute tasks quickly and accurately. Unlike a general-purpose microprocessor, which is designed for a wide range of applications, a microcontroller is specialized for a particular task. This specialization allows for more efficient and dedicated processing, making it ideal for controlling specific functions in various devices. Consider a simple example like a digital thermostat. A microcontroller embedded in the thermostat constantly monitors the temperature and accordingly adjusts it based on pre-set parameters. This precise control not only ensures comfort but also helps conserve energy by efficiently managing the heating or cooling system. Another reason for the increasing popularity of microcontroller is its compact size and low cost, which is especially critical for industrial applications.

It enables the automation and optimization of numerous processes ranging from smart homes to smart cities. In a smart lighting system, for instance, microcontrollers can adjust brightness levels based on ambient light conditions, saving energy and enhancing user experience. Another field where microcontrollers have become extremely popular is robotics, where they serve as the brains behind the mechanical movements and decision-making processes. These devices allow robots to interact with their environment, make real-time decisions, and execute complex tasks with precision.

1.8 Family of Microcontrollers and their Specifications

1.8.1 Brief History of development of 8051 Microcontroller

In the market today, various versions of microcontrollers are available. In order to understand the different families of microcontrollers, it is important to first delve into the history of microcontrollers again. Although TMS1000 is the first microcontroller, which was launched in April 1971, Intel is nonetheless a pioneer in the world of microcontrollers as it introduced a single chip processor Intel 4004 in November 1971 and later, 8-bit 8008 and 8080, which was then perfected as Zilog Z80, one of the best 8-bit microprocessors till date.

In 1976, Intel launched its first microcontroller 8048, an 8-bit architecture, integrating its processing core with memory (code and date) and some other peripherals. It was followed by different derivatives, which came to be known as the MCS-48 family having a wide range of applications such as gaming consoles, control units of car engines and PC keyboards.

In 1980, Intel introduced 8051, an 8-bit microcontroller, the successor of 8048. It became the most popular version of Intel's 8-bit microcontroller, which was later licensed to other manufacturers such as Philips, Siemens and MHS (Matra).Various versions of 8051 were gradually launched and it came to be known as MCS-51 family.

In the coming chapters of this book, 8051 microcontrollers will be mainly discussed and it becomes important to understand the various versions of 8051 and their specifications.

1.8.2 Family of 8051 and their Specifications

Due to the gaining popularity and high demand of 8051, Intel allowed other manufacturers to fabricate and market different variants of 8051. However, it came with a restriction that all these variants should be code compatible with 8051. This resulted in a lot of variants of 8051, among which 8052 and 8031 are the most popular ones and are considered as the family members of 8051. The specifications of these family members can vary, but the basic architecture remains similar across the family. Fig. 1.5 shows a tree containing a family of 8051 along with their specifications.

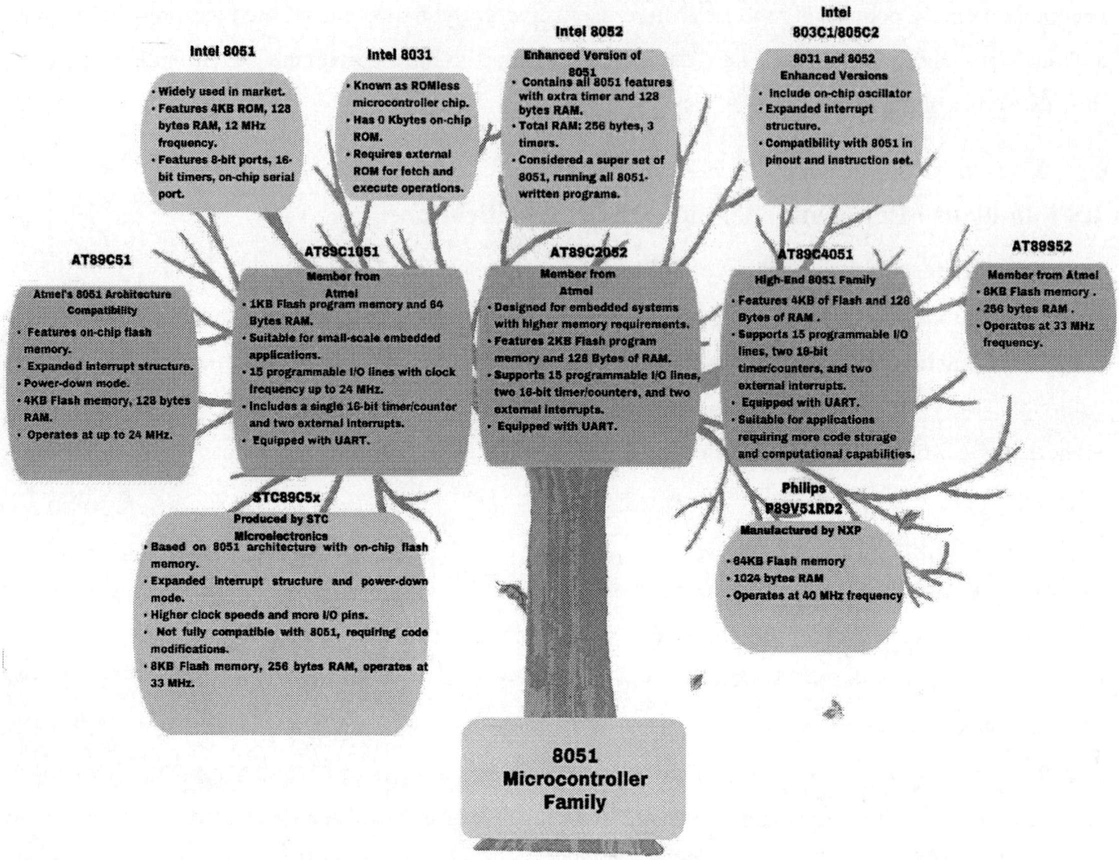

Fig. 1.5 Family Tree of 8051 with Specifications

Some of these are discussed below:

- ***Intel 8051:*** The original 8051 microcontroller was introduced by Intel and became the most widely used microcontroller in the market. It contains a 4KB ROM, 128 bytes of RAM, and operates with a 12 MHz frequency. Other features include four 8-bit ports, two 16-bit timers and one on-chip serial port.
- ***Intel 8031:*** Commonly referred to as ROMless microcontroller chip because it has 0 K byes of on-chip ROM. It requires external ROM for its operation as needed in fetch and execute operations. Apart from this, almost all the features of 8051 are present in 8031.
- ***Intel 8052:*** 8052 is the enhanced version of 8051 containing almost all the features of 8051 with an extra timer and an extra RAM of 128 bytes. Therefore, 8052 has a total of 256 bytes of RAM and 3 timers in all. 8052 is considered as a super set of 8051 as all the programs written for 8051 will run on 8052, but its reverse is not true.
- ***Intel 803C1/805C2:*** These are the enhanced versions of the 8031 and 8052, respectively. They have additional features such as an on-chip oscillator, an expanded interrupt structure, and a power-down mode. In terms of pinout and instruction set, both 803C1 and 805C2 are also compatible with the 8051.

- ***AT89C51:*** A popular member from Atmel, a semiconductor company that acquired the 8051 architecture, the AT89C51 has additional features such as an on-chip flash memory, an expanded interrupt structure, and a power-down mode. Compatible with the 8051 in terms of pinout and instruction set, AT89C51 has 4KB of Flash memory, 128 bytes of RAM, and operates at a frequency of up to 24 MHz.
- ***AT89C1051***

The AT89C1051 is another member of the 8051 microcontroller family produced by Atmel. It contains 1KB of Flash program memory and 64 Bytes of RAM, making it suitable for small-scale embedded applications. With a clock frequency of up to 24 MHz, the AT89C1051 supports a range of external peripherals through its 15 programmable I/O lines. It includes a single 16-bit timer/counter and supports two external interrupts (INT0, INT1). The microcontroller is equipped with a UART for serial communication, providing basic communication capabilities for various applications.

- ***AT89C2052:*** Atmel's AT89C2051 is a versatile microcontroller designed for embedded systems with slightly higher memory requirements. It features 2KB of Flash program memory and 128 Bytes of RAM, providing additional storage capacity compared to the AT89C1051. With a clock frequency of up to 24 MHz, this microcontroller supports 15 programmable I/O lines, two 16-bit timer/counters (T0 and T1), and two external interrupts (INT0, INT1). The inclusion of a UART facilitates serial communication, making it suitable for a broader range of applications.
- ***AT89C4051:*** The AT89C4051 is a higher-end member of the 8051 family, offering increased program memory with 4KB of Flash and 128 Bytes of RAM. With a clock frequency of up to 24 MHz, it provides a robust platform for more complex embedded systems. Similar to its counterparts, the AT89C4051 supports 15 programmable I/O lines, two 16-bit timer/counters (T0 and T1), and two external interrupts (INT0, INT1). The inclusion of a UART ensures seamless serial communication. Its larger program memory makes it well-suited for applications that demand more code storage and computational capabilities.
- ***AT89S52:*** Another member from Atmel, the AT89S52 has 8KB of Flash memory, 256 bytes of RAM, and operates at a frequency of up to 33 MHz.
- ***STC89C5x:*** Produced by STC Microelectronics, this series of member are based on the 8051 architecture but have additional features such as an on-chip flash memory, an expanded interrupt structure, a power-down mode also have higher clock speeds and more I/O pins than the 8051. In terms of pinout and instruction set, they are not fully compatible with the 8051. This requires some modifications in the code to facilitate code migration between them. STC89C52, a popular member of this series has 8KB of Flash memory, 256 bytes of RAM, and operates at a frequency of up to 33 MHz.
- ***Philips P89V51RD2:*** Manufactured by NXP (formerly Philips), this microcontroller has 64KB of Flash memory, 1024 bytes of RAM, and operates at a frequency of up to 40 MHz.

Table 1.2 contains a comparison of the specifications of various versions of 8951.

Table 1.2 Various Versions of 8951

Feature	8051	AT89C1051	AT89C2051	AT89C4051
Program Memory	4KB ROM	1KB Flash	2KB Flash	4KB Flash
Data Memory (RAM)	128 Bytes	64 Bytes	128 Bytes	128 Bytes
Clock Frequency	Up to 12 MHz	Up to 24 MHz	Up to 24 MHz	Up to 24 MHz
I/O Ports	4 I/O Ports	15 I/O Lines	15 I/O Lines	15 I/O Lines
Timers/Counters	2 Timers	1 x 16-bit Timer	2 x 16-bit Timers	2 x 16-bit Timers
Interrupts	6 Interrupts	2 External Interrupts	2 External Interrupts	2 External Interrupts
Serial Communication	UART	UART	UART	UART
Flash Programming Voltage	N/A	12V	12V	12V

UNIT SUMMARY

In this chapter, we delved into the evolution of microcontrollers, tracing their development from their inception to the present day. We explored the fundamental concepts by discussing the block diagram of a microcomputer, highlighting its key elements and functionalities. Furthermore, we examined the differences between Von Neumann and Harvard architectures, discussing their unique characteristics and applications. Additionally, we compared and contrasted microprocessors with microcontrollers, emphasizing their distinct features and roles in various systems. Lastly, we addressed the significance of microcontrollers by explaining the specific needs they fulfill in modern technology, underscoring their versatility and importance in embedded systems and beyond.

KNOW MORE

Father of Microcontroller- Gary Boone

Gary Boone is credited with inventing the first microcontroller-TMS1000 from Texas Instruments in 1971. Gary received his electrical engineering degree from Rose Hulman Institute of Technology in 1967. He went on to Collins Radio in Iowa and then joined Texas Instruments in Houston working in the then-new field of MOS design. He and his team designed custom chips for industrial customers, mostly calculator companies. His projects at TI resulted in the TMX-1795, the world's first 8-bit microprocessor, and the TMS-0100, the first single chip microcontroller. These two pioneering chips were operational in 1971. Based on his work at TI, Gary is listed as inventor on many fundamental microprocessor and microcontroller patents. Gary went on to work for Litronix in Cupertino, Ford Motor Company in Dearborn, UTMC in Colorado Springs and in 1982, he started his own company, Micro Methods, focusing on patent projects and design projects, as a consultant.

EXERCISES

Multiple Choice Questions

1.1 Which of the following is considered the first microcontroller ever developed?

(a) Intel 8080 (b) Motorola 6800

(c) Intel 4004 (d) Zilog Z80

1.2 What was a significant advancement in microcontroller technology during the 1980s that allowed for increased functionality and integration?

(a) Introduction of Flash Memory (b) Adoption of RISC architecture

(c) Development of CMOS technology (d) Integration of Analog-to-Digital Converters

1.3 Which of the following is a characteristic feature of 32-bit microcontrollers that distinguishes them from their 8-bit counterparts?

(a) Lower power consumption (b) Simpler instruction set

(c) Larger address bus (d) Slower clock speed

1.4 What is the primary advantage of using microcontrollers with integrated peripherals in embedded systems?

(a) Reduced power consumption (b) Simplified PCB design

(c) Lower cost (d) Higher clock frequency

1.5 In the evolution of microcontrollers, what does the term "System-on-Chip (SoC) " refer to?

(a) Microcontroller with integrated RAM and ROM

(b) Microcontroller with multiple cores

(c) Integration of microcontroller with other system components on a single chip

(d) Microcontroller with wireless communication capabilities

1.6 What component in the block diagram of a microcomputer is responsible for executing instructions?

(a) ALU (Arithmetic Logic Unit) (b) Control Unit

(c) Memory Unit (d) Input/Output Unit

1.7 In the context of a microcomputer block diagram, where is the temporary storage for data during processing typically located?

(a) Control Unit (b) ALU (Arithmetic Logic Unit)

(c) Memory Unit (d) Input/Output Unit

1.8 Which component manages the flow of data and instructions between the CPU, memory, and input/output devices in a microcomputer?

(a) ALU (Arithmetic Logic Unit) (b) Control Unit

(c) Memory Unit (d) Input/Output Unit

1.9 What is the primary function of the Input/Output Unit in a microcomputer?

(a) Perform arithmetic and logic operations

(b) Store data temporarily during processing

(c) Manage communication with external devices

(d) Control the execution of instructions

1.10 In the microcomputer block diagram, where is the program and data stored for quick access by the CPU?

(a) ALU (Arithmetic Logic Unit) (b) Control Unit

(c) Memory Unit (d) Input/Output Unit

1.11 What is the primary function of the Data Bus in a microcomputer?

(a) Execute instructions

(b) Transfer data between CPU and memory

(c) Manage input devices

(d) Control the flow of information

1.12 Which bus is responsible for carrying control signals to coordinate activities within the microcomputer?

(a) Address Bus (b) Control Bus

(c) Data Bus (d) System Bus

1.13 The bus that carries memory addresses from the CPU to RAM is known as:

(a) System Bus (b) Control Bus

(c) Address Bus (d) Data Bus

1.14 What does the term "width" refer to in the context of a bus?

(a) Physical length of the bus

(b) Speed of data transfer

(c) Number of bits the bus can transmit simultaneously

(d) Type of devices connected to the bus

1.15 Which bus allows different hardware components, such as the CPU, memory, and peripherals, to communicate with each other?

(a) Peripheral Bus (b) System Bus

(c) Input/Output Bus (d) Control Bus

1.16 What is a key characteristic of the Von Neumann architecture?

(a) Separate memory for data and instructions

(b) Parallel processing

(c) Integrated memory for data and instructions

(d) Hierarchical memory structure

1.17 Which architecture uses separate buses for data and instructions?

(a) Von Neumann (b) Harvard

(c) Both A and B (d) None of the above

1.18 In Harvard architecture, what is stored in the program memory?

(a) Only data (b) Only instructions

(c) Both data and instructions (d) Neither data nor instructions

1.19 Which architecture is commonly found in most modern computers and microcontrollers?

(a) Von Neumann (b) Harvard

(c) Both A and B (d) None of the above

1.20 In Von Neumann architecture, what may cause the "von Neumann bottleneck"?

(a) Limited clock speed

(b) Separate memory for data and instructions

(c) Parallel processing

(d) Integrated memory for data and instructions

1.21 What is the primary function of a microprocessor?

(a) Control input and output operations

(b) Execute a set of instructions to perform specific tasks

(c) Manage memory operations

(d) Interface with external peripherals

1.22 Which of the following statements is true regarding microcontrollers?

(a) They only consist of a CPU

(b) They are designed for general-purpose computing

(c) They integrate a CPU, memory, and peripherals on a single chip

(d) They lack input and output capabilities

1.23 In comparison to microprocessors, microcontrollers are more suitable for:

(a) High-performance computing tasks

(b) General-purpose computing

(c) Embedded systems and control applications

(d) Scientific calculations

1.24 Which component is typically found in both microprocessors and microcontrollers?

(a) Only Central Processing Unit (CPU) (b) Memory

(c) Input devices (d) Only Output devices

1.25 What is the primary advantage of using a microcontroller over a microprocessor in certain applications?

(a) Higher processing speed (b) Lower cost and reduced complexity

(c) Larger memory capacity (d) Better multitasking capabilities

1.26 Which of the following is the correct order of the 8051 microcontroller versions in terms of their release?

(a) 8051, 8052, 89C51, 89S52 (b) 89C52, 8051, 89S51, 8052

(c) 8051, 89S51, 8052, 89C52 (d) 89S51, 8051, 89C52, 8052

1.27 What is the major difference between the 8051 and 8052 microcontrollers?

(a) Clock frequency (b) Memory size

(c) Number of I/O ports (d) Instruction set

1.28 Which of the following microcontrollers is an enhanced version of the 8051 with on-chip Flash memory?

(a) 89S52 (b) 89C51

(c) 8051 (d) 8052

1.29 What is the maximum external RAM size that can be interfaced with the standard 8051 microcontroller?

(a) 128 bytes (b) 256 bytes

(c) 512 bytes (d) 1 kilobyte

1.30 Which feature is unique to the 8052 microcontroller compared to the other 8051 variants?

(a) Serial communication (b) On-chip oscillator

(c) Dual data pointers (d) Interrupt handling

Answers of Multiple Choice Questions

1.1 (c) , 1.2 (c), 1.3 (c), 1.4 (b), 1.5 (c) ,1.6 (b) , 1.7 (c), 1.8 (b), 1.9 (c), 1.10 (c), 1.11 (b) , 1.12 (b), 1.13 (c), 1.14 (c), 1.15 (b) ,1.16 (a) , 1.17 (c), 1.18 (b), 1.19 (c), 1.20 (b) ,1.21 (b) , 1.22 (c), 1.23 (c), 1.24 (a), 1.25 (b) , 1.26 (c) , 1.27 (b), 1.28 (a), 1.29 (c), 1.30 (c)

Short and Long Answer Type Questions

Short Answer Questions:

1.1 What is a microcontroller?

1.2 When was the first microcontroller developed?

13. Name a key feature that distinguishes microcontrollers from microprocessors.

1.4 What is the primary function of a microcontroller in electronic systems?

1.5 How has the size of microcontrollers evolved over the years?

1.6 What is the significance of integrating peripherals into microcontrollers?

1.7 Mention one key advantage of using microcontrollers in embedded systems.

1.8 How have advancements in fabrication technology influenced microcontroller development?

1.9 What role did the demand for consumer electronics play in the evolution of Microcontrollers?

Long Answer Questions:

1.10 Trace the historical development of microcontrollers from their inception to the present day. Discuss key milestones.

1.11 Explain the difference between microcontrollers and microprocessors, and highlight scenarios where each is more suitable.

1.12 Describe the impact of Moore's Law on the evolution of microcontrollers.

1.13 Discuss the significance of integrating analog components into modern microcontrollers. Provide examples of applications that benefit from this integration.

1.14 Examine the role of microcontrollers in the Internet of Things (IoT) revolution.

1.15 How have they contributed to the growth of connected devices?

1.16 Explore the challenges faced in the development of microcontrollers, especially in terms of power consumption, performance, and scalability. Analyze the influence of open-source hardware and software on the microcontroller ecosystem.

1.17 Discuss the role of microcontrollers in the automotive industry, highlighting advancements and applications in vehicle systems.

1.18 Explain the evolution of programming languages and development tools for microcontrollers. How have they evolved to simplify the development process?

1.19 Investigate the future trends in microcontroller development, considering factors like energy efficiency, miniaturization, and emerging applications.

2 Architecture of 8051 Microcontroller

UNIT SPECIFICS

This unit elaborately discusses the following topics:

- Salient Features of 8051
- Block Diagram of 8051
- Internal Memory and External Memory
- Internal RAM Structure
- Reset and Clock Circuit
- Various Registers and SFRs of 8051

In order to assess various cognitive skills and encourage a comprehensive understanding of the chapter's content, a variety of multiple choice questions as well as questions of short and long answer types have been included at the end of the chapter. Further, in order to enhance the understanding of the subject among the students, a comprehensive list of references and suggested readings are also given. In various sections, QR codes are available for scanning to access additional supporting information and gather more insights on diverse topics of interest.

RATIONALE

Teaching the architecture of the 8051 microcontroller is crucial for providing a foundational understanding of embedded systems. This knowledge enables students and professionals to grasp the intricacies of designing and programming microcontroller-based applications, fostering competence in embedded system development.

PRE-REQUISITES

Fundamental knowledge of Basic Electronics and familiarity with Boolean algebra, logic gates, and combinational and sequential circuits is essential for understanding the internal workings of the 8051.

UNIT OUTCOMES

After completing the unit, the students will be able to:

U2-O1: Identify the key components and architecture of the 8051 microcontroller.

U2-O2: Describe the memory organization of the 8051, including ROM and RAM.

U2-O3: Develop the ability to design and implement simple input and output interfaces using the available pins on the 8051.

U2-O4: Apply knowledge of the Pin Diagram to design and implement basic applications using the 8051 microcontroller.

U2-O5: Differentiate between general-purpose registers, special function registers, and program status registers.

Unit-2 Outcomes	EXPECTED MAPPING WITH COURSE OUTCOMES (*1- Weak Correlation; 2- Medium correlation; 3- Strong Correlation*)					
	CO-1	CO-2	CO-3	CO-4	CO-5	CO-6
U2-O1	3	-	1	-	-	-
U2-O2	3	1	-	-	-	-
U2-O3	3	2	-	2	-	-
U2-O4	3	2	1	-	-	1
U2-O5	2	2	-	1	-	1

2.1 SALIENT FEATURES OF 8051

The 8051 family is the most popular today, enjoying the majority of the market share. In order to become familiar with the capabilities of 8051, its internal architecture must be studied in detail. It is very important to understand the salient features of 8051 first and then proceed to study its architecture in the next section.

The salient features of 8051 are:

- 8 bit CPU with registers A and B
- Single –bit logic capabilities
- On Chip 4K Program Memory (ROM)
- On Chip 128 bytes Data Memory (RAM)
- Four register Banks, each having eight registers
- 16 bytes addressable at the bit level
- 80 bytes of general purpose data memory
- Bidirectional & individually addressable
- 32 I/O lines arranged as four 8 bit ports: P0-P3
- Two 16-bit timers/counters – T0-T1
- Full duplex UART: SBUF
- 16-bit counter and data pointer (DPTR)
- 8 bit flag register (Program Status Word-PSW)
- Five vector interrupt structure

- On-chip clock oscillator

The oscillator frequency can range between 4-30 MHz, though some versions can run at 33 MHz. The most widely used crystal frequency is 11.0592 MHz to make serial port of 8051 compatible with IBM PC baud rates.

These salient features are studied in further detail after examining the block diagram of the 8051 as shown in Fig.2.1

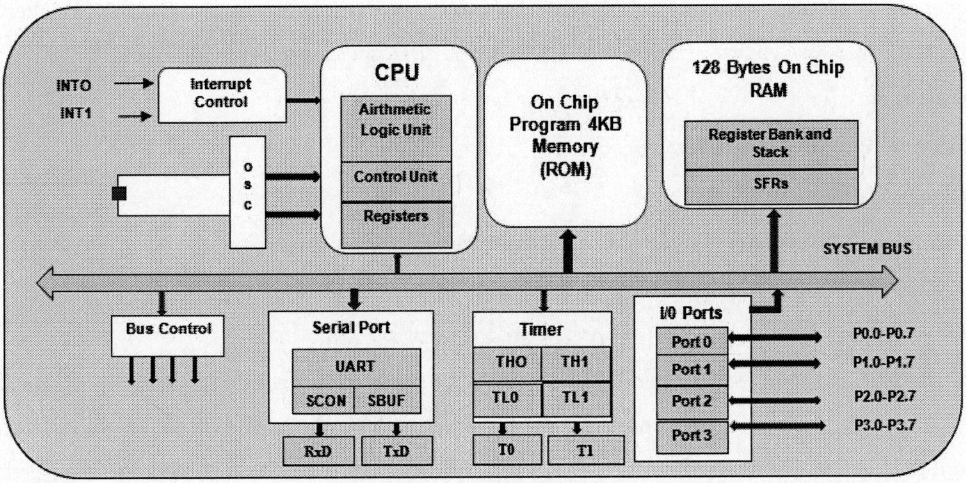

Fig 2.1 8051 Block Diagram

2.2 ARCHITECTURE OF 8051

Let us now study the architecture of 8051 by examining the various blocks one by one.

2.2.1 CENTRAL PROCESSING UNIT (CPU)

CPU is known as the brain of the microcontroller. It monitors all activity in the system and performs all the operations on the data. CPU is mainly a collection of Logic circuits whose main functions is to perform two operations viz. fetching and executing instructions continuously. It includes an arithmetic and Logic unit (ALU), instruction decoder, and timing generator Unit, Accumulator (A), B register and Flag register (PSW).

i. ARITHMETIC AND LOGIC UNIT (ALU)

The Arithmetic and Logic Unit (ALU), as the name suggests, performs various computing functions such as arithmetic and logical operations. In all such operations, the final destination is the accumulator. This means that after the execution of arithmetic and/or logical operations, the final result is stored in the accumulator. This affects the status of various flag bits namely carry (C), Auxiliary Carry (AC), Overflow (O) and Parity (P) of Flag register (also known as Program Status Word). These will be discussed in later sections of this chapter.

ii. Instruction Decoder and Control

After an instruction is fetched from the memory by data bus, it is loaded into the instruction decoder register. The instruction decoder decodes the instruction and decides what action is to be taken. It is a part of the timing and control unit.

iii. Timing Generation Unit

Similar to instruction decoder register, the timing generation unit is also a part of timing and control unit. It generates the various control signals necessary for communication between CPU & peripherals. It is also responsible for synchronization of all microcontroller operations with the clock.

iv. Registers

- **General Purpose Registers**

Accumulator (A) Register

Accumulator is an 8 bit register and is used in all arithmetic and logical instructions. After the execution of these instructions, the final result is stored in accumulator (A) register.

B Register

It is another 8-bit register, widely used in 8051 programming. During multiplication and division operations, B register is used to store one of the 8 bit operands. After the execution of the multiplication instruction, the higher byte of result is stored in B register, whereas lower byte is stored in A register. During division operation, the quotient (integer result of division) is stored in the accumulator (A), while the remainder (leftover after division) is stored in the B register. after the execution. This is shown in Table 2.1.

Table 2.1 Results in Multiplication & Division

Operation	Type	Register A	Register B	Result
Multiplication	byte1 * byte2	Operand 1	Operand 2	A= low byte, B= high byte
Division	byte1/byte 2	Dividend	Divisor	A= Quotient B= Remainder

- **Program Status Word (Flag Register)**

  Flag register in 8051 is also known as Program status word (PSW) and is an 8-bit register. Out of these 8 bits, 6 bits are actually used and 2 are user definable.

  Fig 2.2 shows the various bits of flag register and it can be understood that PSW is a bit addressable register. The register performs both control and status functions. Two flag bits, RSI and RSO determine the current register bank while other flags provide status information. The flag bits of PSW are set or reset after the execution of arithmetic and logic operations.

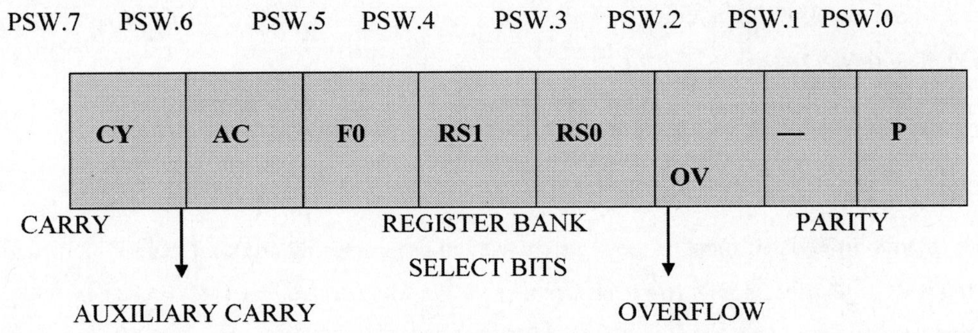

Fig. 2.2 Program Status Word of 8051

Parity (P) Flag (PSW.0)

Parity flag is affected by the number of 1's in the result.

If the result in accumulator contains an even number of 1s, P is reset (P=0).

If the result in accumulator contains an odd number of 1s, P is set. (P=1).

Overflow (OV) flag (PSW.1)

Overflow flag is affected by arithmetic operations involving signed number and is used to detect errors in such operations. OV flag indicates that the sum exceeds the largest positive or negative numbers thought to be needed in the program. After two signed numbers are added, if the result exceeds the destination OV flag is set, else it is reset.

RSI and RSO (PSW 4 and PSW 3)

There are four register banks in 8051 RAM memory. These are register Bank 0, 1, 2 and 3 respectively. Each bank contains eight 8-bit registers R0-R7. By default, register bank 0 is selected. If the user wishes to switch to some other register bank, RS1 and RS0 are used as shown in Table.2.2.

Table 2.2 Register bank Select Bits

RSI	RSO	Register Bank
0	0	Bank 0
0	1	Bank 1
1	0	Bank 2
1	1	Bank 3

The selection of register banks is done by setting or resetting PSW.4 (RS1) and PSW. 3 (RS0) using SETB and CLR single bit instructions. This will be discussed in detail while studying 8051 assembly language programming

Auxiliary Flag (AC)

This flag bit is used in Binary Coded Decimal (BCD) operations. AC is set, if there is a carry from D3 to D4 in the accumulator during addition operation.

Carry (CY) Flag (PSW 7)

Carry Flag is set if a carry is generated in bit D7 of accumulator after an addition operation. Similarly after subtraction, CY is set if borrow occurs else it is reset.

- **8051 16-bit Registers**

Since 8051 is an 8-bit register, most of the registers used in programming are 8-bit general-purpose in nature. However, it also has some 16-bit registers such as Program Counter (PC) and Data Pointer (DPTR), which are mainly used for containing the address bus, which is 16 bit wide. These are discussed below:

Program Counter (PC) Register

The Program Counter (PC) is a special-purpose 16-bit register that holds the memory address of the next instruction to be fetched and executed. After fetching each instruction from the program memory, the PC automatically increments by 1 or by the number of bytes occupied by the instruction, depending on the instruction's size. For example, if an instruction is one byte long, the PC is incremented by 1. If an instruction is two bytes long, the PC is incremented by 2.

Data Pointer (DPTR)

Data Pointer (DPTR) is a 16-bit register that is primarily used for accessing external memory. It consists of two 8-bit registers, DPH (Data Pointer High) and DPL (Data Pointer Low), which together form a 16-bit address. These can also be used as individual 8-bit registers.

By loading appropriate values into DPTR, the data stored in external RAM or ROM can be accessed.

2.2.2 The 8051 Oscillator and Clock

This is basically the heart of the microcontroller and generates clock pulses required for synchronization of all internal operations. Pin nos. 18 (XTAL2) and 19(XTAL1) are used for connecting a resonant network, consisting of a quartz crystal and two capacitors, to form an oscillator (Fig. 2.3).

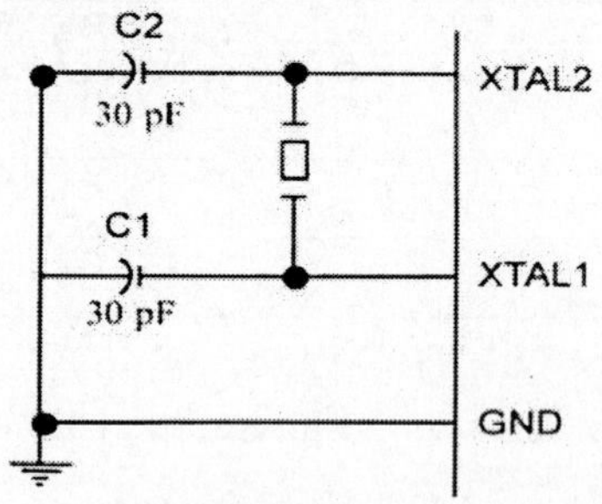

Fig. 2.3 XTAL Connection with 8051

The basic components of the oscillator and clock circuit include:

Crystal Oscillator: The crystal oscillator is a fundamental component in the 8051 clock circuit. It provides a stable frequency for the microcontroller's operation. The crystal is usually connected between the XTAL1 and XTAL2 pins of the 8051. A quartz crystal is typically used for providing the frequency of an oscillator. Ceramic crystals may also be used as a low-cost alternative to quartz crystal. But, in high speed serial data communication or in such operations, where critical timing is required, ceramic crystals suffer from disadvantages of reduced frequency stability and low accuracy. Hence, quartz crystals are the most widely used for resonant circuits.

Capacitors: Two capacitors are connected in parallel with the crystal, one on each side. These capacitors stabilize the crystal oscillations.

Ground Connection: Both sides of the crystal and capacitors are connected to the ground (GND) of the microcontroller.

External Clock Source: Instead of a crystal oscillator, an external clock source can also be used. In this case, the external clock signal is connected to the XTAL1 pin.

Resistor (optional): In some cases, a resistor may be connected in series with the crystal to provide additional stability.

Crystal Frequency:

The crystal frequency is the basic internal clock frequency of the microcontroller. For example, 20 MHz chip must be connected to a quartz crystal with 20 MHz frequency. Though 8051 family microcontrollers can work on a wide range of frequencies ranging from 4 MHz-30 MHz, the most widely used frequency is 11.0592 MHz. Though this way seems to be an odd no. but it is chosen because of band rate compatibility with IBM PCs.

2.2.3 Memory

In Harvard architecture, the memory of 8051 is organized in two parts:

- Program memory (ROM) to store the code
- Data memory (RAM) to store the data

The basic 8051 has 4K on-chip ROM and 128 bytes on-chip RAM. Additional memory can be added externally using circuits.

Internal Data Memory (RAM)

Random access memory (RAM) is volatile memory, which means that it cannot retain data in case of power failure. 8051 has 128 bytes on chip RAM (00-7FH), which is organized into three distinct areas as shown in Fig. 2.4.

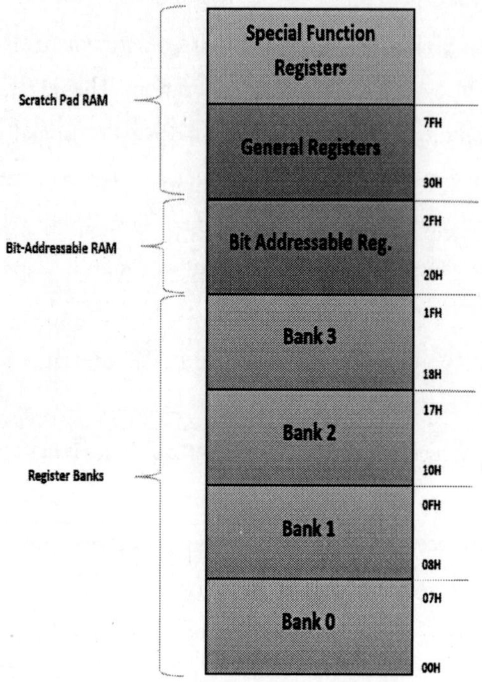

Fig. 2.4 Internal RAM Allocation

(i) Thirty-two bytes from the locations 00-1FH are reserved for four register banks (Bank 0-3) and stack. Each register bank has eight registers (R0-R7) thus making a total of 32 working registers. Each register bank can be addressed by its name or by its RAM addressed by its name or by its RAM address (Fig.2.5).

07	R7	0F	R7	17	R7	1F	R7
06	R6	0E	R6	16	R6	1E	R6
05	R5	0D	R5	15	R5	1D	R5
04	R4	0C	R4	14	R4	1C	R4
03	R3	0B	R3	13	R3	1B	R3
02	R2	0A	R2	12	R2	1A	R2
01	R1	09	R1	11	R1	19	R1
00	R0	08	R0	10	R0	18	R0
	BANK 0		BANK 1		BANK 2		BANK 3

Fig 2.5 Working Registers and their RAM Addresses

On switching on the power supply, register bank 0 is selected by default. Registers R0-R7 refer to working registers of this bank only. However, if the register bank is to be shifted from default register bank 0 to some other register bank, register select bits (RS0 and RS1) of program status word (PSW) are used.

(ii) 8051 supports a special feature allowing access to single bits instead of bytes. It reserves a bit addressable area of 16 bytes from locations 20H to 2FH. It may be noted that bit addressing can also be performed on some of the special function registers (SFRs). Table 2.3 shows bit addresses of internal RAM.

Table.2.3 Bit Addresses of Internal RAM

Byte Addresses	**Bit Addresses**	
	MSB	**LSB**
2F	7F	78
2E	77	70
2D	6F	68
2C	67	60
2B	5F	58
2A	57	50
29	4F	48
28	47	40
27	3F	38
26	37	30
25	2F	28
24	27	20
23	1F	18
22	17	10
21	0F	08
20	07	00

(iii) General purpose RAM area from 30 to 7FH is addressable as bytes. This area is known as scratch pad and is widely used for general purpose data storage.

Note:

Bank 1 and stack use the same RAM space. This poses a major problem in programming the 8051. Care must be taken to either not use register bank 1, or allocate another area of RAM to stack.

Internal Program Memory (ROM)

When 8051 is powered up, the CPU begins execution from location 0 of the program memory. The program memory which is located on the microcontroller chip is known as internal program memory (ROM). It occupies code address space 0000h to FFFFh. The program memory that is located outside the microcontroller chip is called external program memory. Program addresses higher than 0FFFh exceeding the internal ROM capacity, will make 8051 to fetch program bytes from external program memory. There are some situations in which the code bytes are fetched exclusively from the external memory. For example, 8031, a ROM less version of 8051 needs external memory interfacing. This is done by connecting the external access pin(EA), pin number 31 on the DIP, to ground.

Scan to see video on 8051 Architecture

The addresses and functions of various SFRs for 8051 are given in Table 2.4.

Table 2.4 Address and Functions of various SFRs of 8051

S. No.	Name of SFR	Address	Function
1.	Register A (Accumulator)	0xE0	Used for arithmetic and logic operations.
2.	B Register	0xF0	Another 8-bit register used for arithmetic and logic operations, mainly used in multiplication and division operations.
3.	Data Pointer Registers (DPTR)	0x82 (DPL) and 0x83 (DPH)	Used for addressing external memory locations. Together they form a 16-bit address

S. No.	Name of SFR	Address	Function
4.	Program Status Word (PSW)	0xD0	Contains various status bits and flags that reflect the outcome of arithmetic and logical operations. It also contains bits for controlling the arithmetic logic unit (ALU).
5.	Stack Pointer (SP)	0x81	Points to the top of the stack in internal RAM.
6.	Timer/Counter Registers (TMRx)	0x8C (Timer 0 Low Byte), 0x8D (Timer 0 High Byte), 0x8A (Timer 1 Low Byte), 0x8B (Timer 1 High Byte)	Used for timer and counter operations. They can be configured to count internal clock cycles or external events.
7.	Serial Port Control Register (SCON)	0x98	Controls the operation of the serial port (UART) including baud rate, data format, and enabling/disabling serial communication.
8.	Serial Port Data Buffer (SBUF)	0x99	Holds the data to be transmitted or received via the serial port.
9.	Port Registers (P0-P3)	0x80 (P0), 0x90 (P1), 0xA0 (P2), 0xB0 (P3)	Used for interfacing with external devices. Each port can be configured as input or output.
10.	Interrupt Enable Register (IE) and Interrupt Priority Register (IP)	0xA8 (IE), 0xB8 (IP)	IE controls the enabling/disabling of interrupts, while IP determines the priority of interrupts.

2.3 8051 Pin Diagram

The various members of 8051 family come in different packages such as DIP (dual in line package), LLC (leadless chip carrier) and QFP (quad flat package). Although a 20 pin version of the 8051 with a reduced number of I/O ports exists(AT89X051), a majority of companies provide 40 pins versions, having various dedicated functions such as I/O, address, data lines, interrupts, RD, WR, etc. a pin out of the 8051 packaged in a 40 pin DIP is shown in Fig.2.6.

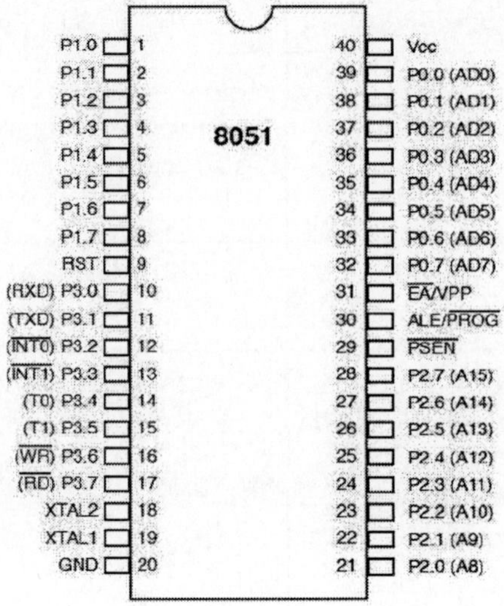

Fig. 2.6 Pin Diagram of 8051 Microcontroller

A notch, as can be seen in Fig.2.6, helps in distinguishing pin number 1 and 40. It can be noted from the pin diagram that out of the 40 pins, a total of 32 pins are reserved for I/O ports P0,P1,P2,P3, each having 8 pins. Except port P1, all other ports have dual functions. Let us now study the functions of each pin.

Pins 1-8 (Port 1)

Pin no. 1-8 of port 1 serve the dedicated input/output function. This is the only port which has no dual function and is used exclusively for I/O as quasi bi directional 8 bit I/O port. Port 1 does not need any external pull up resistors.

Pin 9 (RST)

The RST input pin is the reset input and is used to provide a reset in order to establish initial conditions. A high voltage applied to this pin for two machine cycles will reset the microcontroller. It is a type of non-maskable interrupt.

Table 2.5 Reset Values of SFR

SFR	Value (hex)
PC	0000
DPTR	0000
A	00
B	00
SP	07
PSW	00
P0-P3	FF
IP	XXX0000B
IE	0XX0000B
TMOD	00
TCON	00
TH0	00

SFR	Value (hex)
TL0	00
TH1	00
TL1	00
SCON	00
PCON	0XXXXXXB

The reset values of various SFRs are shown in Table 2.5. It may be noted that the program counter becomes 0 upon reset. This forces the CPU to fetch the first byte of opcode from ROM memory location 0000.

Pins 10-17 (Port 3)

Port 3 is also an input/output port like P1. However, it has dual function of providing some important control signals such as RXD, TXD, RD, WR, T0, T1, INT0, INT1 etc. similar to port1, port 3 does not require external pull up resistors. These alternate functions of P3 are explained below :

Pin 10 (P3.0/RXD)

This is an output pin used for receiving data serially in serial data communication.

Pin 11 (P3.1/TXD)

This is an output pin used for transmitting data serially in serial data communication. RXD and TXD are explained in details in later chapters where serial data communication is discussed in detail.

Pin 12 (P3.2/ INT0)

INT0 stands for external interrupt 0. Input to this pin can set the interrupt flag EE0 in TCON register to 1.

Pin 13 (P3.3/INT1)

INT1 stands for external interrupt 1. Similar to INT0, an input to this pin can set the interrupt flag IE1 in TCON register to 1.

Pin 14 (Pin3.4/T0)

T0 is the timer 0 external interrupt 0, a 16 bit up counter/timer, which is required for counting of external events or generation of precise time delays.

Pin 15 (P3.5/T1)

T1 is the timer external interrupt, similar to timer 0, used for counting of external events or generation of precise time delays.

Pin 16 (P3.6/WR) and Pin 17 (P3.7/RD)

These pins are used for generating control signals such as RD (read) and WR (write). These are active low pins and used in external memory connections.

Pin 18 (XTAL2) and Pin 19 (XTAL1)

These pins are used to provide a resonant circuit consisting of quartz crystal and two capacitors in order to generate internal clock frequency.

Pin 20 (Vss)

Pin 20 is the ground pin.

Pin 21-28 (P2/A8-A15)

Port 2(P2.0-P2.7) is another input/output port having the dual function of providing higher order address lines. Similar to port 1 and 3, port 2 does not require external pull up resistors.

Pin 29 (PSEN)

PSEN, an output pin, is an active low signal and stands for "Program Store Enable". This is connected to the OE (Output Enable) pin of the ROM when external memory is interfaced with 8051.

Pin 30 (ALE/PROG)

ALE(address latch enable) pin is an active high output pin and used to demultiplex lower order address/data lines of port 0 with a 74LS373 latch. It generates a separate set of 8 address lines(A0-A7) by connecting to the G pin of the 74LS373 chip.

Pin 31 (EA/Vpp)

External access (EA) pin is also used in external memory interfacing and cannot be left unconnected. It must be connected to either Vcc or GND. When the on chip is provided with on chip ROM to store programs, EA is connected to Vcc. When external memory is interfaced to ROM less versions of 8051 for example 8031/8032, EA is connected to ground.

Pins 32-39 (P0/AD0-AD7)

Port 0 is a bidirectional I/O port and serves the dual function of providing lower order address and data lines for external memory interfacing. Pin 30 i.e. ALE is used for demultiplexing these address/data lines. when ALE=0,it provides data D0-D7,while when ALE=1,it provides address lines A0-A7. An important point to be noted is that Port 0 requires external pull up resistors of 10k Ohm values, while the other 3 ports have internal pull up resistors.

Pin 40 (Vcc)

The 8051 requires a +5v single power supply with rated current 125mA.

I/O Ports and RESET

Upon Reset, all the ports are configured as inputs. As we have already seen, the status of ports is FF upon reset. When a 0 is written on it, it becomes an output. To reconfigure it as an input port, a 1 must be sent to the port. A real-time picture of an 8051 microcontroller from Philips company is given in Fig. 2.7.

Fig. 2.7 Intel P8051 Microcontroller

UNIT SUMMARY

In this chapter, we delved into the intricate architecture of the 8051 microcontroller, understanding its key components and fundamental organization. We explored the memory structure of the 8051, comprehensively covering both ROM and RAM, and gained insight into how data is stored and accessed within these memory spaces. With a thorough grasp of the Pin Diagram, we can learn to design and execute basic applications leveraging the capabilities of the 8051 microcontroller effectively. Additionally, we developed the ability to discern between general-purpose registers, special function registers, and program status registers, through which we can enhance our proficiency in programming and utilize the 8051 microcontroller to its fullest potential. Through this chapter, we have laid a solid foundation in understanding and harnessing the power of the 8051 microcontroller, equipping ourselves with essential knowledge and skills to embark on more advanced projects and applications.

KNOW MORE

It is interesting to draw a parallel between block diagram of microcontroller and Indian knowledge system:

While IKS emphasizes a holistic view of the world, where every element is interrelated. For example, ancient Indian sciences, like Ayurveda, treat the body as a system where the balance of all elements is essential. Similarly, a microcontroller is designed with various interconnected blocks (e.g., CPU, memory, input/output ports, timers) that work together as a cohesive system to perform specific tasks. Each block must function correctly in relation to the others to ensure the proper operation of the microcontroller.

EXERCISES

Multiple Choice Questions

2.1. What is the primary function of the Central Processing Unit (CPU) in the 8051 microcontroller?

a) Input processing　　b) Data storage

c) Program execution　　d) Output generation

2.2. Which of the following components is responsible for providing the clock signal to the 8051 microcontroller?

a) ALU (Arithmetic Logic Unit)　　b) Timer/Counter

c) Oscillator　　d) RAM (Random Access Memory)

2.3. What is the purpose of the Program Counter (PC) in the 8051 microcontroller?

a) Stores temporary data　　b) Holds address of the current instruction

c) Executes arithmetic operations　　d) Manages input/output operations

2.4. Which part of the 8051 microcontroller is responsible for storing immediate data and intermediate results during arithmetic operations?

a) Stack Pointer (SP) b) Accumulator (ACC)

c) Data Pointer (DPTR) d) Register Bank

2.5. The 8051 microcontroller has how many register banks, and how are they accessed?

a) 1 bank, accessed by R0 and R1

b) 2 banks, accessed by PSW register

c) 3 banks, accessed by bits in PSW register

d) 4 banks, accessed by RS bit in TCON

2.6. Which register is used to control the interrupt system in the 8051 microcontroller?

a) TCON b) IE

c) IP d) PCON

2.7. The 8051 microcontroller's Block Diagram includes a serial communication control block. Which register is associated with serial communication?

a) SBUF b) TCON

c) PSW d) T2CON

2.8. What is the function of the Timer/Counter in the 8051 microcontroller?

a) Count program execution time b) Generate clock pulses

c) Manage interrupts d) Control data input/output

2.9. Which of the following is NOT a part of the 8051 microcontroller's I/O ports?

a) Port 0 b) Port 1

c) Port 2 d) Port 3

2.10. What is the purpose of the PSEN (Program Store Enable) signal in the 8051 microcontroller?

a) Enables external memory

b) Controls the data bus

c) Initiates a program fetch from external memory

d) Manages power supply

2.11. Which block in the 8051 microcontroller's block diagram is responsible for generating the control signals for external memory interfacing?

a) ALU b) Program Memory

c) Data Memory d) Control Unit

2.12. The 8051 microcontroller features a bit-addressable area in which RAM location?

a) 00H b) 20H

c) 80H d) FFH

2.13. What is the function of the Data Pointer (DPTR) in the 8051 microcontroller?

a) Holds address of next instruction b) Stores result of arithmetic operations

c) Points to data in the program memory d) Manages interrupts

2.14. In the 8051 microcontroller, which register is used to control the operation of the Timer/Counter?

a) TCON b) TMOD

c) TL0 d) TH0

2.15. Which block in the 8051 microcontroller's block diagram is responsible for handling external interrupts?

a) Timer/Counter b) Control Unit

c) Interrupt Control d) ALU

2.16. What is the function of the PSW (Program Status Word) register in the 8051 microcontroller?

a) Holds the current instruction address b) Stores result of logical operations

c) Manages the program counter d) Controls program execution flow

2.17. Which block in the 8051 microcontroller is responsible for generating the RST (Reset) signal?

a) Oscillator b) Control Unit

c) Power Supply d) Timer/Counter

2.18. Which of the following addresses corresponds to the special function registers (SFRs) in the Internal RAM of the 8051 microcontroller?

a) 00H to 7FH b) 80H to FFH

c) 00H to 0FH d) 80H to 8FH

2.19. What is the function of the EA (External Access) pin in the 8051 microcontroller?

a) Enables external interrupts b) Controls execution of program

c) Enables external memory access d) Manages power supply

2.20. In the 8051 microcontroller's block diagram, which block is responsible for providing the necessary control signals to synchronize the internal operations?

a) Control Unit b) ALU

c) Timer/Counter d) Data Memory

Answers of Multiple Choice Questions

2.1 (c), 2.2 (c), 2.3 (b) 2.4(b), 2.5 (c) 2.6. (b), 2.7(a) 2.8 (b) 2.9 (d) 2.10 (c), 2.11 (d), 2.12. (c), 2.13 (c) 2.14 (b) 2.15 (c) 2.16 (b) 2.17 (b) 2.18 (b) 2.19 (c), 2.20. (a)

Short and Long Answer Type Questions

Short Answer Questions:

2.1. What is the main function of the ALU in the 8051 microcontroller?

2.2. Name the key components connected to the bus in the 8051 block diagram.

2.3. What role does the Control Unit play in the 8051 microcontroller block diagram?

2.4. How does the 8051 handle interrupts according to its block diagram?

2.5. What is the purpose of the Timer/Counter block in the 8051 microcontroller?

2.6. Which pin of the 8051 microcontroller is designated as the serial data input (RXD)?

2.7. Identify the pin responsible for providing ground (GND) in the 8051 pin diagram.

2.8. What is the function of pin 9 (P3.1/TXD) on the 8051 microcontroller?

2.9. Which pin is associated with external interrupts on the 8051 pin diagram?

2.10. What is the purpose of pin 31 (EA/VPP) in the 8051 microcontroller pin diagram?

Long Answer Questions:

2.11. Explain the basic architecture of the 8051 microcontroller, highlighting the key.

2.12. Describe the purpose of each major block in the 8051 microcontroller's architecture and how they work together to execute instructions.

2.13. Given a specific task, illustrate how the various blocks in the 8051 block diagram collaborate to achieve the desired functionality.

2.14. Investigate the impact of a change in one component of the block diagram on the overall performance of the 8051 microcontroller.

2.15. Devise an improved version of the 8051 microcontroller's block diagram, incorporating modern features or enhancements to address specific application requirements.

2.16. Assess the efficiency of the 8051 microcontroller architecture in comparison to other microcontrollers, considering factors like power consumption, speed, and flexibility.

2.17. Provide a detailed explanation of the pin diagram of the 8051 microcontroller, outlining the functions of each pin.

2.18. Explain how the pin configuration of the 8051 microcontroller contributes to its versatility in interfacing with external devices.

2.19. Design a simple circuit using the 8051 microcontroller and annotate the pin connections, highlighting the purpose of each connection.

2.20. Evaluate the importance of specific pins in the 8051 microcontroller's pin diagram for real-world applications, emphasizing their role in different scenarios.

3 8051 Instruction Set and Programs

UNIT SPECIFICS

This unit elaborately discusses the following topics:

- Overview of 8051 instruction set
- Various addressing modes
- Classification of instructions
- Data transfer instructions
- Arithmetic and Logical instructions
- Branching instructions
- Bit manipulation instructions
- Stack, subroutine and interrupt related instructions

At the end of the chapter, there are different types of questions like multiple choice, short answer, and long answer questions. These questions are meant to help one understand the material better, covering both basic and more advanced concepts. The chapter also provides a list of recommended readings for more information. Plus, there are QR codes the students can scan in different parts of the chapter to find extra helpful resources.

RATIONALE

Learning the 8051 Instruction Set is crucial for understanding microcontroller programming. It helps students gain useful skills that they can use in different types of jobs. It's a hands-on skill that makes them valuable in various fields and helps them contribute to making things better with technology.

PRE-REQUISITES

Familiarity with the general architecture of 8051 microcontroller and its Pin Diagram

UNIT OUTCOMES

After completing the unit, the students will be able to:

U3-O1: Demonstrate the ability to recognize addressing modes of 8051

U3-O2: Understand 8051 Instruction Set

U3-O3: Develop the ability to write assembly language programs for 8051

U3-O4: Apply knowledge of the 8051 instruction set to design embedded systems

Unit-3 Outcomes	EXPECTED MAPPING WITH COURSE OUTCOMES (*1- Weak Correlation; 2- Medium correlation; 3- Strong Correlation*)					
	CO-1	CO-2	CO-3	CO-4	CO-5	CO-6
U3-O1	3	-	1	-	-	-
U3-O2	3	1	-	-	-	-
U3-O3	3	2	-	2	-	-
U3-O4	3	2	1	-	-	1

3.1 Different Programming Languages 8051

After understanding the hardware portion of 8051, it is equally important to learn the software concepts of 8051. Just like we humans need a language to communicate with each other, a microcontroller also needs to be programmed. The various programming languages contain various instructions, also known as codes, to instruct the CPU to perform a desired operation. These instructions are written in the code section of memory by the programmer. The programming languages of 8051 can be broadly categorized as:

- Machine Language
- Assembly Language
- High Level Language

These are discussed in detail in later chapters, but it is important to have a glance at these beforehand.

3.1.1 Machine Language

As the name suggests, machine language stands for the language understood by the machine (microcontroller in this case). A machine code is a group of bits that instruct the CPU to perform a desired operation. These are in forms of 0s and 1s i.e. binary or hexadecimal form. The final code to be burnt into the microcontroller is in this form only. An example of machine language instruction is given here:

00100101 or 25H

This code is for adding a byte of data to the accumulator. Now, imagine if one is to write code in this form of 0s and 1s, how cumbersome the whole procedure will become! This method was followed long back, before the advent of assembly language programming, which is discussed in the next section.

3.1.2 Assembly Language Programming

In order to make programming simpler and easier to write, assembly language was formulated. It uses english-like words, known as mnemonics which are very user friendly and easy to remember. For example, the mnemonic to add data of two registers is ADD A, B. Thus the programmer is eased of the task of remembering machine code for a particular operation. Some other widely used mnemonics are MOV, SJMP, ACALL etc. which will be discussed in greater detail while studying assembly language programming. The programs written in assembly language use the internal registers of microcontroller.

Therefore, it is very important to have a clear knowledge of the arrangement of a particular CPU's internal circuits in order to write the program in assembly language. The programmer writes the program in assembly language in accordance with his convenience. However, ultimately the program is to be converted into a hex file(machine language) in order to burn it in microcontroller memory. A software program, known as assembler, is required to translate the program written in assembly language into machine language.

There are several drawbacks of assembly language programming:

- Since assembly language is hardware specific, the programmer has to be very familiar with the internal hardware of the controller in which the program is to be written.
- Program written for one type of CPU cannot be used for another machine. This means that assembly language programs are not portable.

In order to avoid these drawbacks of assembly language programming, there was a need for another language. This is where the high level languages become advantageous as discussed in next sections.

3.1.3 High Level Languages

High level languages overcome the biggest drawback of assembly language by not being machine specific. In other words, these are portable and the program written for one machine can run on another CPU as well. Various examples of high level languages are PASCAL, BASIC, C, FORTRAN. So a C programmer does not need to be bothered about what microcontroller will be used for the execution of a C program. Out of various programming languages, C is the most popular one for programming a controller because of its several advantages:

- C language is more readable and simpler to write as compared to assembly language. Especially in case of complex applications involving larger codes, assembly language programs become very complex to write.
- Since C is not hardware specific, the programmer does not need to remember all the mnemonics for a particular microcontroller. Hence it is easier to write program in C as compared to assembly language.
- Being a high level language, C has the biggest advantage i.e. it is portable.

Despite several advantages of High Level Language over Assembly Language, it suffers from a major drawback. The machine code (hex file) compiled from a High Level Language program is bigger in size as compared to that created from Assembly Language. The size of the hex file created in either case is very important because microcontrollers have limited on-chip memory.

As we know that ultimately a hex file (machine Language) is to be burnt into the microcontroller, one requires a Software program known as compiler to translate high level language into machine instructions. The program written in a high level language is known as Source program. A compiler translates a source program into object code.

3.2 Overview of 8051 Instruction Set

In the following subsections, we will try to understand the format of writing assembly language and its format.

Instruction Format of MCS-51

The instruction format for MCS-51 is as follows:

Mnemonic, Operand

Mnemonics are abbreviations of the name of the operation being executed. These are basically English-like words, which refer to the operation an instruction performs. For eg. MOV, JMP, INC, ADD etc.

OPERAND defines the data being processed by instructions and forms the second part of instruction. It is quite possible that an instruction may contain no operand at all. For eg. RET. If there is more than one operand in an instruction, they are separated by a comma. For e.g. ADD A, R3. Some instructions may contain more than three operands as well. For e.g. CJE A,#45,AGAIN.

3.3 Various Addressing Modes

Before moving to learning different types of programming instructions, it is important to learn about the various ways by which CPU can access the data, which could be stored in register, or in memory, or can be provided as an immediate value. The various ways of accessing data are called addressing modes, which are determined at the time of design of a microcontroller and cannot be changed by the programmer.

The 8051 supports six addressing modes that allow for flexible manipulation of data and instructions:

1. Immediate Addressing Mode

In this mode, the operand itself is specified directly in the instruction.

For example:

```
MOV A, #10H   ; Move immediate data 10H to accumulator A
```

2. Direct Addressing Mode

In this mode, the address of the operand is directly specified in the instruction. The operand resides in the external RAM of the microcontroller.

For example:

```
MOV A, 30H    ; Move data from external RAM address 30H to accumulator A
```

3. Register Addressing Mode

In this mode, the operand is located in one of the on-chip registers (A, B, R0, R1, ..., R7). For example:

```
MOV A, R0     ; Move data from register R0 to accumulator A
```

4. Register Indirect Addressing Mode

In this mode, the address of the operand is contained in one of the registers, and the data at that address is accessed. For example:

```
MOV A, @R0    ; Move data from the address pointed by R0 to accumulator A
```

5. Indexed Addressing Mode

This mode is used for accessing data from an array or a table in external memory. The address is calculated by adding an offset to a base register. For example:

MOV A, 20H; Move data from external RAM address 20H + DPTR to accumulator A

6. Relative Addressing Mode

This mode is used primarily for conditional branching. The address of the next instruction is calculated relative to the current instruction pointer (PC). For example:

CJNE A, 05H, Label; Compare A with immediate data 05H, if not equal, branch to Label

These addressing modes provide flexibility in accessing data and instructions stored in different locations, allowing programmers to optimize code size and performance for various applications.

3.4 Classification of Instructions

The instructions of the 8051 microcontroller can be classified into following categories based on their functionality and purpose:

- Data Transfer Instructions
- Arithmetic and Logic Instructions
- Branching Instructions
- Bit Manipulation Instructions

In order to understand the various instructions, the list of various operands and their meaning is given in Table 3.1.

Table 3.1 Various Operands used in 8051 Instructions

Operand	Meaning
A	Accumulator
Rn	working registers (R0-R7) , where n=0 to 7
Direct	Any 8-bit address register of RAM, can be any general-purpose register or a SFR
@Ri	indirect internal RAM location addressed by register R0 or R1
#data	An 8-bit constant included in instruction
#data16	A 16-bit constant included as bytes 2 and 3 in instruction (0-65535)
addr16	A 16-bit address, anywhere within 64KB of program memory
addr11	An 11-bit address. May be within the same 2KB page of program memory as the first byte of the following instruction
rel	address of a close memory location (from -128 to +127 relative to the first byte of the following instruction)

3.4.1 Data Transfer Instructions

As the name suggests, Data transfer instructions move the content from one location to another. The name is a bit misleading because the data is only copied and not actually moved because the contents of source are not affected. It may also be noted that the PSW flag register is not affected by these instructions. The various data transfer instructions are MOV, MOVC, MOVX, PUSH, POP and exchange XCHG, XCH instructions as listed in Table 3.2.

Table 3.2 Data Transfer Instructions

DATA TRANSFER INSTRUCTIONS	
Mnemonic	***Description***
MOV A,Rn	Moves the data in register to the accumulator
MOV A,direct	Moves the direct byte to the accumulator
MOV A,@Ri	Moves the indirect RAM to the accumulator
MOV A,#data	Moves the immediate data to the accumulator
MOV Rn,A	Moves the accumulator to the register
MOV Rn,direct	Moves the direct byte to the register
MOV Rn,#data	Moves the immediate data to the register
MOV direct,A	Moves the accumulator to the direct byte
MOV direct,Rn	Moves the register to the direct byte
MOV direct,direct	Moves the direct byte to the direct byte
MOV direct,@Ri	Moves the indirect RAM to the direct byte
MOV direct,#data	Moves the immediate data to the direct byte
MOV @Ri,A	Moves the data at accumulator to the address pointed by Ri
MOV @Ri,direct	Moves the direct byte to the indirect RAM
MOV @Ri,#data	Moves the immediate data to the indirect RAM
MOV DPTR,#data	Moves a 16-bit data to the data pointer
MOVC A,@A+DPTR	Moves the code byte relative to the DPTR to the accumulator (address=A+DPTR)
MOVC A,@A+PC	Moves the code byte relative to the PC to the accumulator (address=A+PC)
MOVX A,@Ri	Moves the external RAM (8-bit address) to the accumulator
MOVX A,@DPTR	Moves the external RAM (16-bit address) to the accumulator
MOVX @Ri,A	Moves the accumulator to the external RAM (8-bit address)
MOVX @DPTR,A	Moves the accumulator to the external RAM (16-bit address)
XCH A,Rn	Exchanges the register with the accumulator
XCH A,direct	Exchanges the direct byte with the accumulator
XCH A,@Ri	Exchanges the indirect RAM with the accumulator
XCHD A,@Ri	Exchanges the low-order nibble indirect RAM with the accumulator

3.4.2 Arithmetic and Logical Instructions

Arithmetic instructions perform several basic arithmetic operations such as addition, subtraction, division, multiplication etc. After execution, the result is always stored in the accumulator. It may be noted that the status of the PSW register is affected by arithmetic and logic operations. MCS-51 supports 8-bit arithmetic unsigned operations although it is possible to carry out signed operations by using overflow flag (OV). The various instructions are ADD, ADDC, SUBB, INC, DEC MUL, DIV and DAA as shown in Table 3.3.

Table 3.3 Arithmetic and Logical Instructions

ARITHMETIC INSTRUCTIONS	
Mnemonic	***Description***
ADD A,Rn	Adds the register to the accumulator
ADD A,direct	Adds the direct byte to the accumulator
ADD A,@Ri	Adds the indirect RAM to the accumulator
ADD A,#data	Adds the immediate data to the accumulator
ADDC A,Rn	Adds the register to the accumulator with a carry flag
ADDC A,direct	Adds the direct byte to the accumulator with a carry flag
ADDC A,@Ri	Adds the indirect RAM to the accumulator with a carry flag
ADDC A,#data	Adds the immediate data to the accumulator with a carry flag
SUBB A,Rn	Subtracts the register from the accumulator with a borrow
SUBB A,direct	Subtracts the direct byte from the accumulator with a borrow
SUBB A,@Ri	Subtracts the indirect RAM from the accumulator with a borrow
SUBB A,#data	Subtracts the immediate data from the accumulator with a borrow
INC A	Increments the accumulator by 1
INC Rn	Increments the register by 1
INC Rx	Increments the direct byte by 1
INC @Ri	Increments the indirect RAM by 1
DEC A	Decrements the accumulator by 1
DEC Rn	Decrements the register by 1
DEC Rx	Decrements the direct byte by 1
DEC @Ri	Decrements the indirect RAM by 1
INC DPTR	Increments the Data Pointer by 1
MUL AB	Multiplies A and B
DIV AB	Divides A by B
DAA	Decimal adjustment of the accumulator according to BCD code

Logical Instructions include bitwise operations such as AND, OR, EXOR, CLR, CPL, Rotate and SWAP instructions. Logical instructions may contain two 8-bit operands. Some examples are AND, OR and XOR for e.g. ANL A,R1. Then there may be single operand instructions such as CLR, CPL, ROTATE and

SWAP. It may be noted that not all logical instructions affect the PSW register. Table 3.4 lists some logical instructions.

Table 3.4 Logic Instructions

LOGIC INSTRUCTIONS	
Mnemonic	**Description**
ANL A,Rn	AND register to accumulator
ANL A,direct	AND direct byte to accumulator
ANL A,@Ri	AND indirect RAM to accumulator
ANL A,#data	AND immediate data to accumulator
ANL direct,A	AND accumulator to direct byte
ANL direct,#data	AND immediate data to direct register
ORL A,Rn	OR register to accumulator
ORL A,direct	OR direct byte to accumulator
ORL A,@Ri	OR indirect RAM to accumulator
ORL direct,A	OR accumulator to direct byte
ORL direct,#data	OR immediate data to direct byte
XRL A,Rn	Exclusive OR register to accumulator
XRL A,direct	Exclusive OR direct byte to accumulator
XRL A,@Ri	Exclusive OR indirect RAM to accumulator
XRL A,#data	Exclusive OR immediate data to accumulator
XRL direct,A	Exclusive OR accumulator to direct byte
XORL direct,#data	Exclusive OR immediate data to direct byte

All mnemonics copyrighted © Intel Corporation 1980

3.4.3 Branching Instructions

Branching instructions are used in those situations, when it is necessary to transfer the program control to a different location during the execution of a program. These may be broadly classified as JUMP and CALL and Return(RET) instructions.

JUMP Instructions are of further two types:

- Conditional JUMP
- Unconditional JUMP

Conditional JUMP

As the name suggests, conditional jump instruction is executed only if some condition is satisfied, otherwise it will simply ignore the same and move to the next instruction. Table 3.5 lists some conditional jump instructions.

Table 3.5 Conditional Jump Instructions

CONDITIONAL JUMP INSTRUCTIONS	
Mnemonic	**Description**
JC Label	Jump if carry flag is set
JNC Label	Jump if carry flag is not set
JB bit, Label	Jump if direct bit is set
JBC bit, Label	Jump if direct bit is set and clears bit
JZ, Label	Jump if the accumulator is zero
JNZ, Label	Jump if the accumulator is not zero
CJNE A,direct	Compares direct byte to the accumulator and jumps if not equal
CJNE A,#data	Compares immediate data to the accumulator and jumps if not equal
CJNE Rn,#data	Compares immediate data to the register and jumps if not equal
CJNE @Ri,#data	Compares immediate data to indirect register and jumps if not equal
DJNZ Rn,r Label	Decrements register and jumps if not 0
DJNZ Rx, Label	Decrements direct byte and jump if not 0

Let us take the example of JC instruction: JC, Label

```
        JC, HERE
        MOV P1,#55H
        MOV A,P1
HERE:MOV A,#0AAH
```

Unconditional JUMP

As the name suggests, Unconditional jump transfers the control to the target unconditionally. Mainly there are two types of conditional jumps

- Long Jump (LJMP)
- Short Jump (SJMP)

These are discuss below:

Long Jump (LJMP)

LJMP is a 3-byte unconditional jump, in which the first byte represents the opcode, while the second and third byte represents the 16-bit address of the destination. The 16-bit target address enables a jump to any memory location ranging from 0000 to FFFFH.

Short Jump (SJMP)

SJMP is a 2-byte unconditional jump, in which the first byte represents the opcode, while the second byte represents the relative address of the destination, enabling a jump to any memory location ranging from 00 to FFH. It may be noted here that this address range is divided into forward and backward jump. If the jump is forward, the target location can be within a memory space of 127 bytes from the current Program Counter value. Similarly, If the jump is backward, the target location can be within a memory space of -128 bytes from the current Program Counter value. Thus the total relative address of the target location is within -128 to +127.

It is also worth mentioning here that in addition to SJMP, all conditional jumps are also short jump instructions since these are also 2-byte instructions.

Concept of Looping in 8051

Sometimes, a certain task is to be repeated many times in a program. In such cases, the concept of looping is used. A loop can be defined as repeating a sequence of instructions a particular number of times.

In the 8051 microcontroller, the loop is performed by using the instruction "DJNZ reg, label". Before the execution of the loop, a value, known as counter, is loaded into the register (any register of R0-R7), for the number repetitions of the task. When the loop starts, it first decrements the register by 1 and then checks the status of the register. If it is not zero, it jumps to the target address of the label. The loop ends once the value of register reaches zero and the next instruction is executed.

It may be noted that in DJNZ instruction, two operations viz. register decrement and the decision to jump are combined in a single instruction. This saves memory in addition to saving the tedious task of repetition.

The other branching instructions- CALL and RET are discussed in subsequent subsections while discussing subroutine related instructions.

3.4.4 Bit Manipulation Instructions

Many times, it is required to access only 1 or 2 bits of the ports instead of the entire 8 bits. The 8051 microcontroller is capable of accessing individual bits of the port without altering the rest of bits in that particular port. This powerful feature of 8051 is known as bit addressability. In fact, 8051 was one of the first microcontrollers to have a dedicated boolean architecture which made it exceptionally fast while processing a single bit.

The syntax of a single bit is PX.Y, where X is port number 0,1,2,3 while Y is the bit number from 0 to 7 for data bits D0 to D7. Here D0 is the Least Significant Bit (LSB) while D7 is the Most Significant Bit (MSB). One point to be remembered is that since D0 represents the 1st bit, D1 will represent the second bit and so on.

For example, P1.0 represents the first bit (D0) of port 1. Similarly P1.7 represents the 8th bit (D7) of port 1.

SETB Instruction

The instruction used for accessing a single bit of a port and turning it high is SETB PX.Y, where X is port number 0,1,2,3 while Y is the bit number, which is to be accessed. For example, SETB P0.1 is used to set the bit 1 of port 0 high i.e. logic 1.

CLR Instruction

The instruction used for accessing a single bit of a port and turning it low is CLR PX.Y, where X is port number 0,1,2,3 while Y is the bit number, which is to be accessed. For example, CLR P0.1 is used to set the bit 1 of port 0 low i.e. logic 0.

CPL Instruction

The CPL instruction changes the value of a certain destination to its opposite. It basically complements the value i.e. if a bit was 1, it becomes 0, and if it was 0, it becomes 1. Let us take a few examples to understand this instruction:

CPL C ; Compliments the bit stored in Carry flag

If the carry flag previously contained 1, it becomes 0

CPL can also be used to complement the registers or memory addresses

CPL A ; Compliments the bits stored in register A

For example, if register A contains 55H i.e. 01010101 B,

CPL A will convert 0s into 1 and 1s into 0 i.e 01010101 B now becomes 10101010B or AAH.

3.4.5 Stack Related Instructions

Since there are a limited number of registers in 8051, the CPU needs a storage area, which can store data temporarily during the operation of the microcontroller. The stack refers to a section of the internal RAM area of 8051, which stores information (either data or address) temporarily.

Accessing Stack using Stack Pointer (SP) Register

8051 uses an 8-bit register known as Stack Pointer (SP) register to access the stack area. Stack Pointer is used to hold an internal RAM address where the last byte of data was stored. SP plays a very important role whenever the data is to be stored on the stack or retrieved from the stack. When the data is to be placed on the stack, the SP increments by 1 and then data is stored on the stack. When the 8051 microcontroller is powered up or reset, the SP register is set to 07H. This implies that the first location used for the stack by the 8051 is 08H as the SP register gets incremented first before storing the data. The reverse happens when the data is retrieved from the stack. The byte is first read from the stack and then the SP register decrements to point to the next available byte of stored information.

Please note that this operation is different from microprocessors, particularly x86 processors, in which the SP is decremented when the data is stored on the stack.

Default value of the SP register is 07H when the 8051 is reset and can be changed by the programmer using MOV instruction studied earlier. Also, it can be noted that internal RAM locations 08 to 1F i.e 24 bytes can be used for the stack. However, if the programmer needs to use more than 24 bytes of stack, MOV instruction can be used to change the SP to point to RAM locations 30-7FH only. This is because internal RAM locations 20 to 2FH are reserved for bit-addressable memory and cannot be used by the stack.

PUSH and POP Instructions

Storing data in the stack is known as PUSH and retrieving the data off from the stack is known as POP.

Example: PUSH R5

On execution of this instruction, SP is incremented by 1 and contents of R5 are stored in location 08H.

Similarly, the operation of POP instruction can be understood by following example:

Example: POP R3

On execution of this instruction, the top byte of stack is copied into register R3 and SP is decremented by 1.

These instructions will be understood in more detail in the last part of this chapter, where examples will be taken to explain the instructions.

3.4.6 Subroutine Related Instructions

During the execution of a program, if a particular task is to be performed many times, subroutines are used to organize and optimize the code. A subroutine is basically a small program consisting of a set of instructions, which are written outside the main program. Subroutines help break down a large program into smaller, more manageable modules. Each subroutine can be designed to perform a specific task, such as reading sensor data, performing calculations, or controlling output devices. Once a subroutine is written and tested, it can be reused multiple times throughout the program. This reduces redundancy and saves both time and memory.

Some of the commonly used subroutine related instructions are given below:

CALL Instruction

It is another type of control transfer instruction and is also used to call subroutines located anywhere within the 64 Kbyte memory address in 8051. The call is used to transfer control to the starting address of the target subroutine. Depending upon the target address, there are two types of CALL instructions:

- LCALL (long call)
- ACALL (absolute or short call)

(i) ***LCALL (long call)***

It is a 3 byte instruction, in which the first byte is opcode, while the second and third byte contain the 16-bit address of target subroutine. Hence, LCALL is used to call the subroutine located anywhere in the 64 Kbyte address program memory space.

(ii) ACALL (Absolute Call)

In this 2-byte instruction, only 11-bits of 2 Bytes are used thus, making the specified target address range within 2 Kbytes.

Hence, the main difference between ACALL and LCALL is that the target address in ACALL instruction must be within 2 KByte, while that in LCALL is anywhere within the 64 Kbyte address program memory space of the 8051.

Role of Stack in CALL instructions

As we have discussed, a CALL instruction transfers the control to the target address of the subroutine. After executing the subroutine, the program must return to the main program and resume operation. Since, the subroutine may be located anywhere within the program memory space of the 8051, the stack area of internal RAM is used to store the address of the next instruction after the CALL. When a CALL is encountered, the CPU immediately stores the Program Counter (PC) on the stack, the control is transferred to the new location and the subroutine is executed.

RET (RETURN) Instruction

At the end of every subroutine, RET instruction is used to transfer the control back to the main program, which pops the address from the stack into the Program Counter (PC) and thus returns back to the instruction immediately after the CALL instruction.

Scan here to watch video on 8051 programming

3.4.7 Interrupts

In the 8051 microcontroller, an interrupt is a mechanism that allows the microcontroller to respond to internal conditions or external events immediately without waiting for the completion of the current instruction. On encountering an interrupt, the microcontroller temporarily suspends its current operation, saves the current state of execution, and jumps to a predefined location in memory called an Interrupt Service Routine (ISR) in order to handle the interrupt. In the 8051 microcontroller architecture, interrupt-related instructions are used to handle interrupts efficiently.

There are two main types of interrupts in the 8051 microcontroller- Hardware Interrupts and Software Interrupts.

- ***Hardware Interrupts***

These interrupts are triggered by external hardware events such as a timer overflow, external interrupt pins (INT0 and INT1), serial communication, or other peripheral devices. When a hardware interrupt occurs, the microcontroller jumps to the corresponding ISR to handle the event.

Hardware Interrupt Related Instructions

Some interrupt-related instructions for hardware interrupts in the 8051 include:

- ***EI (Enable Interrupts)***

After a system reset or when acknowledging an interrupt, the EI instruction is used to enable interrupts. This resets the Interrupt Enable flip-flop, which initially disables interrupts. This instruction enables interrupts globally. Once enabled, the microcontroller responds to interrupt requests.

- ***DI (Disable Interrupts)***

The DI instruction is used to disable interrupts when a code sequence must run without interruption. For instance, it's used at the start of critical time delays, with interrupts re-enabled at the end of the code. This instruction disables interrupts globally. When interrupts are disabled, the microcontroller ignores any interrupt requests.

- ***Software Interrupts***

Unlike hardware interrupts, software interrupts are triggered by specific instructions within the program code. In the 8051 architecture, there aren't specific instructions for software interrupts as in some other architectures. Instead, software interrupts can be created by utilizing particular memory locations and jump instructions.

Overall, interrupt-related instructions in the 8051 are essential for controlling how the microcontroller responds to outside events and for handling important tasks promptly.

Some notes on programming must be kept in mind, while writing a program:

Notes on Programming:

- # Sign is used to indicate data. If there is no # sign, it indicates memory value. For example MOV A, #25H indicates value 25H is to be loaded into register A, while MOV A,25H indicates value from memory location 25H will be loaded into register A.
- H stands for hexadecimal and is mostly used while using assembly language. For example #55H indicates hexadecimal data with 55 value.
- If the data starts with alphabets from A to F, a 0 will be used after # and the letter to indicate that it is a hex number and not a letter.
- The source and destination should be of the same size. If a value larger than the register is moved, it will cause an error. For example, instruction MOV A,#2345 will cause an error as register A is only 8-bit while immediate value 2345 is 16-bit wide.
- @pointer can be used for pointing to some memory address.

3.5 Various Directives of Assembly Language Programming

Assembly Language Directives direct the assembler Program what to do during the process of Assembling even though they are written in the Mnemonic field of the program. These are not the instructions to the 8051 Microcontroller Assembler and are actually instructions to the Assembler. These directives do not translate directly into machine code but control the assembly process and are essential for creating efficient and well-structured programs. Some of the commonly used directives in 8051 assembly language programming are:

1. ORG (Origin)

This directive sets the starting address for the program or a section of the program. For example ORG 0000H tells the assembler to assemble the next statement at 0000H.

2. END

This directive marks the end of the source code and any text following this directive is ignored by the assembler.

3. DB (Define Byte)

This directive is used to define an 8-bit data byte or bytes.

For example DATA1 DB 0AH, 0BH, 0CH defines three bytes with values 0x0A, 0x0B, and 0x0C.

4. DW (Define Word)

This directive is used to define a 16-bit data word or words.

For example DATA2 DW 1234H defines a word with the value 0x1234.

5. EQU (Equate)

This directive is used to define a constant value that can be used throughout the program.

6. DATA

This directive indicates that the following section of code is data memory.

7. BIT

This directive is used to define bit-addressable memory locations.

For example: MY_BIT BIT 10H defines a bit at address 0x10.

By using these directives, programmers can effectively manage the code and data organization, ensuring that the 8051 microcontroller executes the intended instructions accurately.

3.6 Programs Based on 8051 Instructions and Assembler Directives

As we have seen from earlier subsections, each instruction in the 8051 instruction set does a specific job and helps the microcontroller run programs and control external devices. After understanding the various instructions for 8051, let us take some examples to understand their functionalities in detail.

3.6.1 Programs Based on Data Transfer Instructions

As studied in earlier sections, data can be copied to either register or memory location. Sometimes, the data also needs to be transferred from external memory to internal memory and vice-versa with the help of MOVX instruction. Another point worth mentioning is that although the instruction says move, the contents are not actually moved, they are only copied. This means that the source is not affected with the execution of mov instruction, only the destination is affected. The following examples illustrate the various applications of data transfer instructions.

Example 3.1 Write a program to transfer data 63H into register R0 and then transfer the contents to register A.

Solution: This is a simple program, which makes use of MOV(move) instruction. The program is given below:

```
ORG 0000          ; Start the program at address 0
MOV R0, #63H      ; Move immediate data 63H to R0
MOV A, R0         ; Move data from register R0 to  accumulator  A
END               ; End of program
```

Explanation: The program begins with ORG instruction, which sets the location of program memory to 0000. MOV R0, #63H is used to copy immediate data value 63H into register R0. Instruction MOV A, R0 data from register R0 to accumulator A. The END instruction marks the end of the program.

Example 3.2 Write a program to move data from memory location 63H into register R0 and then transfer the contents to register A.

Solution: The program is given below:

```
ORG 0000          ; Start the program at address 0
MOV R0, 63H       ; Move the data contained in memory location 63H to R0
MOV A, R0         ; Move data from register R0 to  accumulator  A
END               ; End of program
```

Explanation: The program begins with ORG instruction, which sets the location of program memory to 0000. MOV R0, #63H is used to copy immediate data value 63H into register R0. Instruction MOV A, R0 data from register R0 to accumulator A. The END instruction marks the end of the program.

Example 3.3 Write a program to move data from internal memory location 25H to another RAM location 52H

Solution: This is a simple program to move data within internal RAM to another RAM location.

```
ORG 0000          ; Start the program at address 0
MOV 52H, 25H      ; Move contents of RAM location 25H to RAM location 52H
END               ; End of program
```

Explanation: The program begins with ORG instruction, which sets the location of program memory to 0000. Instruction MOV 52H, 25H copies the contents of RAM location 25H to RAM location 52H.

Example 3.4 Write a program to move data from memory location pointed by register R1 to register R2 in 8051. Use the DPTR register.

Solution:

```
ORG 0000            ; Start the program at address 0
MOV DPTR, R1        ; Load the address pointed by R1 into DPTR
MOVX A, @DPTR       ; Move data from the memory location pointed by DPTR to Accumulator
MOV R2, A           ; Move the data from Accumulator to R2
END                 ; End of program
```

Explanation: To move data from the memory location pointed by register R1 to register R2 in the 8051 microcontroller, the address pointed by R1 is to be loaded into the Data Pointer (DPTR). Then the data from the memory location pointed by DPTR is to be moved to the Accumulator (A). and finally the data from the Accumulator (A) is to be moved to register R2.

Example 3.5 Write a program to copy data from external source memory location (5000 H) to destination memory location (6000 H).

Solution: Since the data cannot be copied directly from one memory location to another, it has to be first copied to register A with the help of DPTR register. The program is given below:

```
ORG 0000            ; Start of program memory
MOV DPTR, #5000H    ; Load DPTR with the source memory address 5000H
MOVX A, @DPTR       ; Move data from source memory to accumulator
MOV DPTR, #6000H    ; Load DPTR with the destination memory address 6000H
MOV @DPTR, A        ; Move data from accumulator to destination memory
END                 ; End of program
```

Explanation: The program begins with ORG instruction, which sets the location of program memory to 0000. The instruction MOV DPTR, #5000H copies values 5000H into the DPTR register. Please note the # sign, which indicates that it is a value. Thus DPTR now points to source memory location 5000H. Then using MOVX A, @DPTR, the data is copied from source memory (5000H) to the accumulator. Next, the instruction MOV DPTR, #6000H loads DPTR with the destination memory address 6000H and finally MOV @DPTR, A copies the data from accumulator to destination memory. The END instruction marks the end of the program.

Notice the use of MOVX and DPTR for copying contents from external memory source to internal memory.

3.6.2 Programs Based on Arithmetic Instructions

As discussed in earlier sections, 8051 has a variety of arithmetic instructions for performing arithmetic operations. Let us now study some programs, which utilize these instructions.

An important point to be remembered is that all arithmetic operations are performed on the accumulator i.e the destination for all arithmetic operations has to be accumulator only and no other general-purpose register.

Example 3.6 Write a program to add immediate data 34H to accumulator.

Solution: This is a simple program, which adds the accumulator (A) with the operand specified in the source. The program is given below:

```
ORG 0000          ; Start of program memory
ADD A, #34H       ; adds 34H data to accumulator
END               ; End of program
```

Example 3.7 Write a program to add the value stored in register R0 to the accumulator.

Solution:

```
ORG 0000          ; Start of program memory
MOV A, #10        ; Move10 value to accumulator
MOV R0, #20       ; Move 20 value to register R0
ADD A, R0         ; Adds the value in register R0 to accumulator A
END               ; End of program
```

After the execution of this program, the value contained in R0 register i.e. 10 will be added to that in the accumulator, which contains 20. And hence, finally the accumulator will contain 10+20 i.e. 30.

Example 3.8 Write a program to add the value stored at the address pointed by the R0 register to the accumulator (A).

Solution: Since this program involves the address pointed by register R0, pointer@ will be used.

```
ORG 0000          ; Start of program memory
MOV R0, #30H      ; Copy value 30H to register R0
ADD A, @R0        ; Adds the value at address 30H to accumulator A
END               ; End of program
```

Explanation: This program is an example of indirect addressing mode. Here the address is not directly mentioned but indirectly using a pointer. Initially, 30H is added as an immediate value to R0. However, when a pointer is used with Ro, the value contained in R0 becomes an address (30H) and CPU automatically points to 30H memory location. Whatever value is stored in that address will be added to the accumulator using ADD A,@R0.

Note how the usage of pointer@ before R0 changes the whole operation of the program. Now instead of adding the value contained in R0, it will add the value contained in the address pointed by R0.

Example 3.9 Write a program to increment accumulator, register R1 and then add their contents.

Solution: This is a simple program, which makes use of INC instruction.

```
ORG 0000          ; Start of program memory
MOV A, #20        ; Copy value 20 to accumulator
```

```
MOV R1, #30        ; Copy value 30 to register R1
INC A              ; Increment accumulator by 1
INC R1             ; Increment register R1 by 1
ADD A, R1          ; Adds the value at R1 to accumulator A
END                ; End of program
```

Explanation: After the execution of INC instruction the values in accumulator and register R1 are incremented by 1 and become 21 and 31 respectively. At the end of the program, these values are added and the accumulator finally contains 21+31 i.e. 52.

Example 3.10 Write a program to multiply the contents of accumulator with register B and store the results in memory location 56H.

Solution:

```
ORG 0000           ; Start of program memory
MOV A, #5          ; Copy value 5 to accumulator
MOV R1, #30        ; Copy value 30H to register R1
MUL A,B            ; Multiply contents of B with A
MOV 56H, A         ; Copy the contents of A to memory location 56H
END                ; End of program
```

3.6.3 Programs Based on Logical Instructions

Logical operations in the 8051 microcontroller perform bitwise operations between the accumulator and data stored in a memory location, register, or data given by the programmer. The result of a logical operation is stored in the accumulator itself.

Example 3.11 Write a program to perform the logical AND operation between FFH and 0FH and store the result in port P1.

Solution:

```
ORG 0000           ; Start of program memory
MOV A, #0FFH       ; Load value FFH into accumulator
ANL A, #0FH        ; Perform logical AND operation on FFH with 0FH
MOV P1, A          ; Store result in Port 1
END                ; End of program
```

Explanation: After execution of AND operation, the accumulator will contain 0FH and then the result is stored in Port P1. Notice the use of 0 before immediate value FH as it will indicate data.

Example 3.12 Write a program to perform the logical AND operation between FFH and 0FH and store the result in port P1.

Solution:

```
ORG 0000            ; Start of program memory
MOV A, #0FH         ; Load value 0FH into accumulator
ANL A, #0F0H        ; Perform logical OR operation on 0FH with F0H
MOV P1, A           ; Store result in Port 1
END                 ; End of program
```

Explanation: After execution of OR operation, the accumulator will contain FFH and then the result is stored in Port P1. Notice the use of 0 before immediate value FH as it will indicate data.

Similar programs can be written for performing XOR, NOT operations and it is worthwhile mentioning here that similar to Arithmetic operations, all logical operations are also performed on accumulator and the final result is stored in the accumulator itself.

3.6.4 Programs Based on Branching Instructions

Branching instructions in 8051 assembly enable the program to jump to specific parts of the code depending on conditions. These control the program flow with both conditional and unconditional jumps. As seen earlier, these instructions check the contents of the accumulator/ Flag bits and accordingly change the sequence of the program to some other location, whose address is given by Label.

Example 3.13 Write a program to check if the contents of R1 is 0. If yes, send the contents to R2, else send FFH to R0.

Solution:

```
ORG 0000            ; Start of program memory
MOV A, R1           ; Copy the contents of R1 into A
JZ HERE             ; if A=0, jump to location HERE
MOV R0, #0FF        ; if A is not 0, send FFH to R0
HERE: MOV R2, A     ; Copy the contents of A to R2
END                 ; End of program
```

Explanation: This program makes use of JZ conditional instruction. The instruction MOV A, R1 first copies the contents of R1 into A. Then the condition of A is checked using JZ HERE. If it is zero, the program is transferred to the label HERE using JZ HERE. If it is not zero, the contents of the accumulator are copied into R2.

Example 3.14 Write a program to add two numbers FFH and 0AH. If a carry is generated, send 0000 to R1, else send FFH to R4.

Solution:

The same program can be executed using either JC or JNC. Both programs are given below and there is a slight change in the logic.

(i) Using JC Instruction

```
ORG 0000H           ; Start address
```

```
MOV A, #0FFH          ; Load accumulator A with FFH
MOV B, #0AH           ; Load register B with 0AH
ADD A, B              ; Add contents of B to A
JC  NEXT              ; Jump to NEXT if there is a carry
MOV R4, FFH           ; If there is no carry, continue execution here
NEXT: MOV R1, 00H     ; If there is a carry, execution jumps here
END                   ; End of program
```

Explanation: In this program, the carry flag (CY) in the flag register (PSW) is utilized to determine if a jump to label NEXT is to be made or not. First the two numbers FFH and 0AH are copied to registers A and B respectively using MOV instructions. Then these are added using instruction ADD A, B. After the addition, the condition of the CY flag is checked and the decision to jump to label NEXT is made using JC instruction. If a carry is generated, the program control is transferred to Label NEXT using JC, else the next instruction is executed.

(ii) Using JNC Instruction

```
ORG 0000H             ; Start address
MOV A, #0FFH          ; Load accumulator A with FFH
MOV B, #0AH           ; Load register B with 0AH
ADD A, B              ; Add contents of B to A
JNC  NEXT             ; Jump to NEXT if there is no carry
MOV R1, 00H           ; If there is carry, continue execution here
NEXT: MOV R4, FFH     ; If there is no carry, execution jumps here
END                   ; End of program
```

Explanation: In this program, there is a slight change from the earlier one. Here, the decision to transfer control to label NEXT is made using JNC. If a carry is not generated, the program control is transferred to Label NEXT using JNC, else the next instruction is executed.

Example 3.15 Write a program to add 2 to register A 100 times using looping.

Solution:

```
ORG 0000H             ; Start address
MOV A, #0             ; Initialize register A to 0, clear Accumulator
MOV R1, #100          ; add multiplier 100 to R1
LOOP:  ADD A, #02     ; Add 2 to register A
DJNZ R1, LOOP         ; Decrement R1 and jump to LOOP if R1 is not zero
END                   ; End of program
```

Explanation: This program makes use of the concept of looping using DJNZ instruction. Initially, the accumulator is initialized to 0 using MOV A, #0. Then, the multiplier 100 is moved to R1, thus making it a counter. The loop begins with label LOOP, which adds 02 to accumulator, decrements R1 and is repeated 100 times till the register R1 reaches 0. Once this condition is reached, the loop ends and the next instruction is executed.

Input/Output State of Ports

In 8051 architecture, the pull-up resistors are enabled by default upon reset. This means that when you configure a port pin as an input and do not drive it explicitly to a logic low state, it will be internally pulled up to Vcc (logic high). Any port can be made an input by sending FFH i.e 11111111 to it, while it can be made output by sensing 0000 to its bits.

Example 3.16 Suppose a real byte of data is being received at Port P1. Write a program to send this data to P2.

Solution:

```
ORG 0000H          ; Start address
MOV P1,#0FFH       ; Make port P1 an input port
MOV A,P1           ; Send the data received at P1 to accumulator
MOV P2, A          ; Send data at accumulator to P2
END
```

Explanation:

In this Program, first the port 1 is made an input port by sending data 11111111 to all its bits and making them high. Now, it may be remembered that data cannot be sent directly from one port to another, it is first sent to the accumulator by instruction MOV A,P1 and then using instruction MOV P2, A, it is sent to port P2.

Machine Cycle in 8051

Each Instruction takes some time to be executed in terms of clock cycles known as machine cycles in 8051. Depending upon the frequency of quartz crystal connected on pin 18 and 19 as well as chip manufacturer, the length of clock cycle varies. Normally a clock frequency of 11.0592 MHz is used for 8051 microcontrollers as the baud rate compatibility is best at this clock frequency. Also, a prescaler or divider of 12 is used in some architectures, which means one machine takes 12 Oscillator periods). Thus, the frequency is first divided by 12 and then its reverse is calculated to obtain the machine cycle.

Delay Subroutine

Since each instruction has its own machine cycles, the time taken to execute the instructions can be used to generate the time delay. Normally, DJNZ instruction is used for creating a delay subroutine. We have already seen the use of DJNZ for creating a loop earlier. This can be understood further with the help of an example program.

Example 3.17 Write a program to blink alternate LEDs connected to port P2 with some delay.

Solution:

```
ORG 0000H                ; Start address
MOV P2, #0000            ; Make P2 an output port
MOV P2, #55H             ; Make alternate LEDs connected to
P2 ON
ACALL DELAY              ; give delay by going to DELAY subroutine
MOV P2, #0AAH            ; Toggle the LEDs connected to P2
ACALL DELAY
END
DELAY: MOV R1,#200       ; Load R1 with 200 counter value
HERE: DJNZ R1, HERE      ; Stay here till R1 becomes 0
RET                      ; Return to main program
```

Explanation:

In this program, 8 LEDs are connected to port P2 and hence, it is made an output port by making all bits high. Then alternate LEDs connected to P2 are turned on by sending 55H (01010101B) to P2. A delay subroutine is called ACALL DELAY instruction, which changes the control of the program to the subroutine. A delay is generated by first moving a counter value 200 into R1. DJNZ instruction decrements R1 and keeps on repeating till R1 becomes 0. Once this condition is fulfilled, it moves to next instruction RET, which takes the control back to main program. Then instruction MOV P2, #0AAH (10101010B) toggles the LEDs. Again Delay subroutine is called, executed and the program ends.

SCAN ME

3.6.5 Programs Based on Bit Manipulation Instructions

As discussed earlier, bit manipulation instructions in 8051 allow us to manipulate individual bits within registers and memory locations. The single bit addressability of 8051 is an advantage over microprocessors, where the whole byte is to be changed instead of a single bit. Also, the ports can be addressed individually, if need be. In assembly language, each port pin is written as P0.0, P0.1 and so on. Before understanding the programs based on bit manipulation instructions, it is important to understand some points regarding the port structure of 8051.

Pull up Resistors in 8051 Port Structure

The 8051 microcontroller typically supports an internal pull-up resistor feature for its I/O ports, allowing for convenient interfacing with external devices, particularly switches and other digital input devices. The pull-up feature ensures that when an input pin is not actively driven to a logic high state (i.e., when no external signal is applied), the pin is internally pulled up to a logic high level (Vcc). However, Port 0 is an exception to this and requires external pull up resistors as it does not have internal pull up resistors. This is called open-drain and is shown in Fig. 3.1.

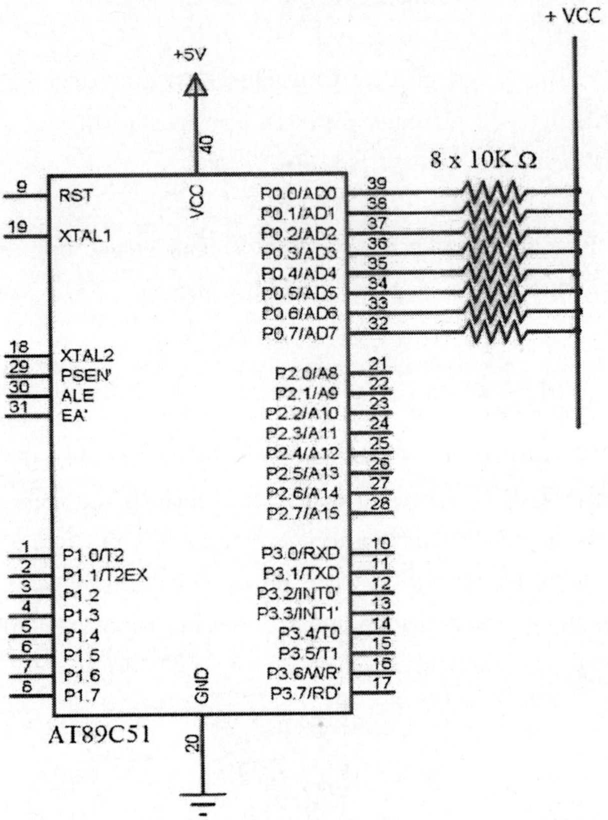

Fig 3.1 Open Drain in 8051 Requiring External Pull-up Resistors

So when a bit is set high by SETB instruction, it is connected to Vcc, while when it is cleared by CLR instruction, it is connected to ground.

Let us now learn assembly language programming based on bit manipulation instructions.

Example 3.18 Write a program to set bit P1.0 high and then clear it.

Solution:

```
ORG 0000H        ; Start address
SETB P1.0        ; Turn on bit P1.0
CLR P1.0         ; Clear bit P1.0
END              ; end the program
```

Explanation:

This program makes use of the single bit instructions SETB and CLR, where SETB P1.0 makes the bit P1.0 high, while CLR instruction turns it off.

Example 3.19 Write a program to make bit P1.0 high and then complement it.

Solution:

```
ORG 0000H          ; Start address
SETB P1.0          ; make bit P1.0 high
CPL P1.0           ; complement bit P1.0
END                ; end the program
```

Explanation:

This program makes use of the single bit instruction CPL, which changes the state of the bit. In this program since the state of bit P1.0 is made high by STB P1.0, the CPL will change its state to 0.

Example 3.20 Write a program that sends a high-to-low pulse to pin P1.5 whenever a sensor connected to pin P2.3 detects an input.

Solution:

```
ORG 0000H                    ; Start address
SENSOR_PIN EQU P2.3          ; Define P2.3 as SENSOR_PIN
OUTPUT_PIN EQU P1.5          ; Define P1.5 as  OUTPUT_PIN
SETB SENSOR_PIN              ; Enable P2.3 as input pin
CLR OUTPUT_PIN               ; Make P1.5 as output pin
HERE: JNB SENSOR_PIN HERE    ; Wait here till P2.3 is low
SETB OUTPUT_PIN              ; Set P1.5 high
ACALL DELAY                  ; Give a small delay
CLR OUTPUT_PIN               ; Set P1.5 low
ACALL DELAY                  ; Give a small delay
SJMP HERE                    ; Repeat indefinitely
DELAY: MOV R1,#200           ; Load R1 with 200 counter value
HERE:  DJNZ R1, HERE         ; Stay here till R1 becomes 0
RET                          ; Return to main program
```

Explanation: This program uses EQU directive for defining pin numbers and assigning them names. The advantage of using this directive is that if at some point , the programmer wants to change the pin numbers, it has to be done only initially while defining, because in the rest of the program, only names will be used. So, initially EQU defines Pin 2.3 and Pin 1.5 as SENSOR_PIN and OUTPUT_PIN respectively. Then these pins are made input and output by using SETB SENSOR_PIN and CLR OUTPUT_PIN respectively. JNB SENSOR_PIN HERE instruction keeps checking for P2.3; till it remains low, the program remains there itself. The moment this condition becomes false, i.e it detects an input and becomes high, the next instruction SETB OUTPUT_PIN sets P1.5 high, ACALL DELAY gives a small delay followed by CLR OUTPUT_PIN, which sets P1.5 low.

3.6.6 Programs Based on Stack, Subroutine and Interrupt Related Instructions

Let us now discuss some programs related to stack, subroutines and interrupt related instructions.

Example 3.20 Write a program to load FFH on R0, push its content on stack, load AAH on R1, push its content on stack, retrieve contents of R1 to R2 and those of R0 to R3.

Solution:

```
ORG 0H              ; Start address of the program
MOV R0, #0FFH       ; Load a value into R0
PUSH R0             ; Push R0 onto the stack
MOV R1, #0AAH       ; Load another value into R1
PUSH R1             ; Push R1 onto the stack
POP R2              ; Pop the top value of the stack into R2
POP R3              ; Pop the next value of the stack into R3
END
```

Explanation: This program demonstrates basic stack operations in assembly language for the 8051 microcontroller. It loads values into registers R0 and R1, then pushes them onto the stack. It then pops the values from the stack into registers R2 and R3, respectively.

Example 3.21 Write a program to add 10H to accumulator, call a subroutine to save contents of accumulator on stack, add contents of memory location pointed by register R0 to accumulator, retrieve contents from stack back to accumulator.

Solution:

```
ORG 0000H           ; Start of program memory
MOV A, #10H         ; Load accumulator with value 10H
CALL SUB_ROUTE      ; Call subroutine
END
SUB_ROUTE:
PUSH ACC            ; Save accumulator on the stack
MOV A, #05H         ; Load accumulator with value 05H
ADD A, @R0          ; Add value at address pointed by R0 to accumulator
POP ACC             ; Restore accumulator from the stack
RET                 ; Return from subroutine
```

UNIT SUMMARY

In this chapter, we delved into the instruction set of the 8051 microcontroller, understanding various addressing modes. We gained insight into how instructions are classified. With a thorough understanding of the instruction set, we can learn to write programs for 8051 microcontroller effectively. Through this chapter, we have laid a solid foundation in assembly language programming of the 8051 microcontroller, equipping ourselves with essential knowledge and skills to embark on more advanced projects and applications.

KNOW MORE

All microcontrollers, which are compatible with 8051 contain a total of 255 instructions. This means that a total of 255 different words are available for program writing. At first instance, it seems a bit difficult to consider that so many numbers have to be learnt by heart. However, It is not as complicated as it seems to be. In actuality, there are only 111 truly different commands. This is because many instructions are considered to be "different", even though they perform the same operation.

EXERCISES

Multiple Choice Questions

3.1 What is the size of the memory space in the 8051 microcontroller?

(a) 1 KB (b) 2 KB

(c) 4 KB (d) 8 KB

3.2 Which register is used for storing data in the 8051 microcontroller?

(a) A (b) B

(c) DPTR (d) R0

3.3 Which instruction is used to clear a register in the 8051 assembly language?

(a) CLR (b) MOV

(c) CLR A (d) CLR C

3.4 Which flag is set when an arithmetic operation results in a carry out of the MSB in the accumulator?

(a) CY (b) AC

(c) OV (d) P

3.5 What is the function of the CJNE instruction in 8051 assembly language?

(a) Compare and jump if not equal (b) Compare and jump if equal

(c) Compare and jump if carry (d) Compare and jump if not carry

3.6 What is the role of the PCON register in the 8051 microcontroller?

(a) Program Counter (b) Power Control

(c) Port Configuration (d) Processor Configuration

3.7 Which addressing mode is used for immediate addressing in 8051 assembly language?

(a) Register addressing (b) Direct addressing

(c) Indirect addressing (d) Immediate addressing

3.8 Which register pair is used for indirect addressing in the 8051 microcontroller?

(a) R0-R1 (b) R2-R3

(c) R4-R5 (d) DPTR

3.9 Write the assembly code to add two numbers stored in registers R0 and R1 and store the result in R2?

(a) MOV A, R0 / ADD A, R1 / MOV R2, A

(b) ADD A, R0 / ADD A, R1 / MOV R2, A

(c) MOV A, R0 / ADD R1, A / MOV R2, A

(d) MOV A, R0 / ADD A, R2 / MOV R1, A

3.10 How many bytes does the SJMP instruction occupy in memory?

(a) 1 byte (b) 2 bytes

(c) 3 bytes (d) 4 bytes

3.11 Which instruction is used to set a bit in the SFR (Special Function Register) in the 8051 microcontroller?

(a) SETB (b) MOV

(c) CLR (d) ORL

3.12 What is the purpose of the INC instruction in 8051 assembly language?

(a) Increment the accumulator (b) Increment a register

(c) Increment the program counter (d) Increment the stack pointer

3.13 Which register is commonly used as the stack pointer in the 8051 microcontroller?

(a) SP (b) DPTR

(c) R7 (d) R6

3.14 What are the differences between CALL and ACALL instructions in 8051 assembly language?

(a) CALL can only call subroutines within the same bank, while ACALL can call subroutines in any bank.

(b) CALL is used for unconditional jumps, while ACALL is used for conditional jumps.

(c) CALL is a 2-byte instruction, while ACALL is a 3-byte instruction.

(d) CALL can only jump to a location within the same 256-byte page, while ACALL can jump to any location.

3.15 When would you use the CJNE instruction instead of the DJNZ instruction in 8051 assembly language?

(a) When comparing two numbers (b) When decrementing a counter

(c) When looping through an array (d) When checking for overflow

3.16 What are the advantages of using indirect addressing mode in 8051 assembly language?

(a) Allows access to larger memory spaces (b) Simplifies complex calculations

(c) Increases program execution speed (d) Reduces code size

Answers of Multiple Choice Questions

3.1(c), 3.2(a), 3.3(c), 3.4(a), 3.5(a), 3.6(b), 3.7(d), 3.8(d), 3.9(a), 3.10(b), 3.11(a), 3.12(b), 3.13(a) 3.14(c) 3.15(a) 3.16(d)

Short and Long Answer Type Questions

Short Answer Questions

3.17 Define the purpose of the Accumulator (ACC) register in the 8051 microcontroller.

3.18 Explain the function of the CJNE instruction in 8051 assembly language programming.

3.19 Describe the role of the PSW (Program Status Word) register in the 8051 microcontroller.

3.20 Differentiate between direct addressing mode and indirect addressing mode in 8051 assembly language.

3.21 What is the purpose of the MOV instruction in 8051 assembly language programming?

3.22 Briefly explain the function of the INC instruction in 8051 assembly language.

3.23 Define the purpose of the SJMP instruction in 8051 assembly language programming.

3.24 Explain how the CLR instruction is used to clear a register in 8051 assembly language.

3.25 What is the significance of the DPTR (Data Pointer) register in the 8051 microcontroller?

3.26 Describe the function of the RET instruction in subroutine execution in 8051 assembly language.

Long Answer Questions

3.27 Discuss the steps involved in initializing the 8051 microcontroller and configuring its ports for I/O operations.

3.28 Explain the concept of subroutine implementation in 8051 assembly language programming, including the use of CALL and RET instructions.

3.29 Describe the process of performing multiplication and division operations in 8051 assembly language, considering the limitations of the microcontroller.

3.30 Discuss the advantages and disadvantages of using direct addressing mode and indirect addressing mode in 8051 assembly language programming.

3.31 Discuss the use of bit manipulation instructions such as SETB and CLR in 8051 assembly language programming, with examples.

3.32 Describe the process of implementing conditional branching and looping constructs in 8051 assembly language programming.

3.33 Explain the significance of the stack in subroutine execution on the 8051 microcontroller, including stack pointer management.

4 Embedded C Programming of 8051

UNIT SPECIFICS

This unit elaborately discusses the following topics:

(i) Data Types for 8051

(ii) Syntax for Embedded C Programming

(iii) Example Programs in C for 8051

Towards the chapter's conclusion, various question formats such as multiple choice, short answer, and long answer are included. These inquiries aim to enhance comprehension, addressing fundamental as well as advanced concepts. Additionally, the chapter offers a compilation of suggested readings for further insight. Moreover, students can utilize QR codes dispersed throughout the chapter to access supplementary resources.

RATIONALE

Learning Embedded C programming for the 8051 microcontroller is important because it equips a student with valuable skills for controlling and managing electronic devices. With Embedded C, one can write programs that make gadgets like microwave ovens, remote controls, and even car systems work smoothly. Understanding how to program the 8051 microcontroller gives a student the power to create smart and efficient devices, enhancing your ability to innovate and solve real-world problems in fields like electronics, robotics, and automation.

PRE-REQUISITES

Familiarity with the general architecture of 8051 microcontroller and its Pin Diagram

UNIT OUTCOMES

After completing the unit, the students will be able to:

U4-O1: Understand the syntax and structure of the C programming language in the context of embedded systems.

U4-O2: Able to write efficient Embedded code for solving real world problems.

U4-O3: Develop skills to design, implement, and debug embedded software for various applications.

U4-O4: Practice troubleshooting techniques to identify and rectify errors in embedded C programs.

Unit-4 Outcomes	EXPECTED MAPPING WITH COURSE OUTCOMES (1- Weak Correlation; 2- Medium correlation; 3- Strong Correlation)					
	CO-1	CO-2	CO-3	CO-4	CO-5	CO-6
U4-O1	3	-	1	-	-	-
U4-O2	3	1	-	-	-	-
U4-O3	3	2	-	2	-	-
U4-O4	3	2	1	-	-	1

4.1 Different Programming Languages of 8051

As discussed in the previous chapter, the various programming languages of 8051 can be broadly categorized as:

- Machine Language
- Assembly Language
- High Level Language

We have already discussed the assembly language and various instruction sets related to development of programs based on assembly language for 8051. Assembly language is much simpler and easier to write as it uses English-like words, known as mnemonics which are very user friendly and easy to remember. However, there are several drawbacks of assembly language programming:

- Since assembly language is hardware specific, the programmer has to be very familiar with the internal hardware of the controller in which the program is to be written.
- Programs written for one type of CPU cannot be used for another machine. This means that assembly language programs are not portable.

In order to avoid these drawbacks of assembly language programming, high level language such as Embedded C language was developed by the programmers. High level languages overcome the biggest drawback of assembly language by not being machine specific. In other words, these are portable and the program written for one machine can run on another CPU as well. So a C programmer does not need to be bothered about what microcontroller will be used for the execution of a C program. Out of various programming languages, C is the most popular one for programming a controller because of its several advantages:

- C language is more readable and simpler to write as compared to assembly language. Especially in case of complex applications involving larger codes, assembly language programs become very complex to write.
- Since C is not hardware specific, the programmer does not need to remember all the mnemonics for a particular microcontroller. Hence it is easier to write programs in C as compared to assembly language.
- Being a high level language, C has the biggest advantage i.e. it is portable.

In this chapter, Embedded C programming for 8051 will be studied in detail covering the various data types, syntax for Embedded C programming and various C language programs.

4.2 Data Types for 8051 C

There are various data types for 8051 C programming similar to general C programming. Some of the most widely used data types are discussed in this section.

4.2.1 Char Data Type

Char, short form for character data type, is the most widely used data type for 8051 microcontrollers, which are also 8-bit wide. It is mainly of two types:

- Unsigned Char
- Signed Char

Unsigned Char is an 8-bit data type, has a value in the range of 0-255 (00-FFH) and typically takes up 1 byte of memory. It is very popular especially for situations such as setting a counter value.

Signed Char is mainly used for those applications, where negative sign is required and has a value in the range of -128 to +127. It is the default data type for char, if unsigned keyword is not used in front of char.

4.2.2 Int Data Type

Int, short form for integer data type, is a 16-bit data type and is used to store integers. In 8051 C, an int typically occupies 2 bytes of memory. In those situations, where a counter of value more than 255 is required, char data type cannot be used as it has an upper limit of 255. In such situations, int data type can be used. Similar to char data type, int is also mainly of two types:

- Unsigned int
- Signed int

Unsigned int is a 16-bit data type that has a value in the range of 0 to 65535 (0000 -FFFFH). It is mainly used to define 16-bit variables such as memory addresses and gives a wide range of data declaration.

Signed int is mainly used for those applications, where negative sign is required and has a value in the range of -32768 to +32767. It is the default data type for int, if unsigned keyword is not used in front of int.

It may be kept in mind that since int data type uses 2 bytes of data, the use of this data type must be done carefully only where it is required. For example, for a data value like 100, bit char and int can be used since it comes in the range of both data types. However, the on-chip memory of 8051 is limited, usage of 16-bit int will unnecessarily consume 1 extra byte of memory than char. So, although the compiler will not generate any error in such a case, a larger hex file will be generated.

4.2.3 Sbit Data Type

S bit, short form for Single bit, is a popular data type for 8051 and is used specifically for accessing single-bit registers. It is mainly used to access the single bits of SFRs, especially the bit-addressable ports P0-P3. An important point to be remembered about sbit data type is that it should be declared globally i.e. outside the main program. This will be discussed further in the upcoming sections, where C programming is discussed.

4.2.4 Bit Data Type

The bit data type is used to define a single bit variable for accessing the bit addressable memory section of 20 - 2FH. The main difference between bit and sbit data types is that while sbit is used for bit-addressable SFRs, the bit data type is used for the bit-addressable memory section of 20-2FH.

4.2.5 SFR and Float Data Types

SFR is used to access the byte-size SFR registers, while float data type is used to store floating-point numbers. Due to the lack of a built-in floating-point unit in 8051, float is slower and less precise compared to integers.

Some of the widely used data types for 8051 C are shown in Table 4.1.

Table 4.1 Data Types for 8051 C

Sr. No.	Data Type	Size (Bits)	Data Range
1.	CHAR • Unsigned Char • Signed Char	 • 8-bit • 8-bit	 • 0 to 255 • -128 to +127
2.	INT • Unsigned Int • Signed Int	 • 16-bit • 16-bit	 • 0 to 65535 • -32768 to +32767
3.	sbit	1-bit	SFR bit-addressable only
4.	bit	1-bit	RAM bit-addressable only
5.	sfr	8-bit	RAM addresses 80- FFH only

SCAN HERE TO LEARN MORE ABOUT EMBEDDED C

4.3 Syntax for 8051 C Programming

The syntax for 8051 C programming is very similar to standard C programming, with some specific considerations due to the architecture and features of the 8051 microcontroller. The C programming syntax mainly consists of the following components:

1. Comments

Comments are used to increase the readability of the program and are normally ignored by the compiler. One can use `//` for single-line comments and `/* */` for multi-line comments, just like in standard C.

2. Preprocessor Directives

Preprocessor directives are used to include header files and define constants.

In 8051 C programming, header files play a crucial role in organizing the code, declaring functions, and defining constants specific to the 8051 microcontroller. The most commonly used header file for 8051 microcontrollers is <reg51.h>. This header file provides access to register definitions and special function register (SFR) declarations, allowing to directly manipulate hardware peripherals and registers of the 8051 microcontroller.

```
#include <reg51.h> // Include 8051-specific header file
#define LED P1^0   // Define LED pin
```

3. Data Types

We have already studied the data types such as char, int, float, etc., along with 8051-specific data types such as sbit earlier. With the exception of sbit, most of the data types are defined in the main body of the program.

4. Functions

Functions in 8051 C programming follow the standard C syntax.

```
eg      void myFunction()
 {
    // Function body
 }
```

5. Main Function

The main function is the entry point of the program. It must return void. The main body of program is written following the main function as given below:

```
void main()
{
   // Main function body
}
```

6. Looping Constructs

Standard C looping constructs like while, for, do-while loops are used for certain conditions. Some examples are:

```
while (condition)
{
   // Loop body
}
for (initialization; condition; increment/decrement) {
   // Loop body
```

```
}
do
{
    // Loop body
} while (condition);
```

These are some of the key syntax elements in 8051 C programming. Keep in mind that the specific syntax and features may vary slightly depending on the compiler and development environment being used.

SCAN HERE TO LEARN MORE ABOUT EMBEDDED C

4.4 Points to Remember in 8051 C Programming

There are some points, which need to be kept in mind while programming in C for 8051. These are given below:

(i) Every program must begin with a header file. For example #include<reg51.h> is used as a header file for 8051 family of microcontrollers.

(ii) Single bits are represented by ^ symbol. For example, bit 0 of port P1 is represented as P1^0.

(iii) In order to repeat a process continuously, while(1) or for(;;) is used.

(iv) To assign a value a single = is used, while for comparing == is used.

(v) Main program is written in void main (void) after curly bracket starts.

(vi) To generate a delay "for" loop is used with statement terminator ";", while in order to create a loop "for" statement is used without any terminator.

(vii) Sbit is declared globally i.e. before start of main program.

(viii) When a subroutine is used, it must also be declared first before the main program.

(ix) Comments improve the readability of the program and must be included in the program by using "//".

(x) In order to make a port as input, all bits should be made high by sending value FF, similarly value 00 must be send to make the port output.

(xi) In C, hexadecimal value is represented by writing 0x before the value. For example, FFH is represented as 0xFF in C.

(xii) Suitable data types must be used to assign names to variables.

(xiii) #define can also be used to define ports or their pins. For example #define LED P1 is used to define port P1 by name LED. Whenever LED will be used in the program, it will automatically consider P1.

(xiv) When the header file is not used, sfr can be used to access ports. SFR data type is another way to access the SFR RAM space 80-FFH.

The various addresses of ports are shown in Table 4.2.

Table 4.2 Addresses of 4 Ports

Port	Address
P0	80H or 0x80
P1	90H or 0x90
P2	A0H or 0xA0
P3	B0H or 0xB0

4.5 Programs Based on Embedded C for 8051

After studying the various data types and syntax of Embedded C programming for 8051, let us now study some programs using 8051 C involving various data types.

Example 4.1 Write an 8051 C program to add two numbers 50 and 100 and send the result to port P1.

Solution:

```
#include <8051.h>
void main()
{
   unsigned char num1 = 100;// Assign first number as num1
   unsigned char num2 = 50;  //Assign second number as num2
   unsigned char result;                //declare result variable for storing result
   result = num1 + num2;                // Add num1 and num2
   P1 = result;                 // Output result to port P1
}
```

Explanation: This program uses two character data types and assigns variable names as num1 and num 2 to 100 and 50 respectively. Since the two numbers lie in the range of 0-255, unsigned char data type has been used. Another variable result has been declared using unsigned data type to store the result of addition. The numbers are added and the result is sent to P1 using P1= result.

Example 4.2 Write an 8051 C program to check if a number is positive or negative. If it is positive, send 55H to P1 else send AAH to P2.

Solution:

```
#include <8051.h>
void main()
{
```

```
signed char num          // Initializing a signed char variable
// Checking whether the variable is positive or negative
if (num >= 0)
    {
  // The variable is positive
  P1=0x55;
    }
else
    {
  // The variable is negative
   P2=0xAA;
    }
 while(1);               // Infinite loop to halt the program
}
```

Explanation: This program begins with assigning a signed char data type to variable num. Then the variable is compared with zero. If it is greater than or equal to zero, it means it is positive and P1 is assigned with value 55 H, else it is negative and P2 is assigned AAH. Please note that in Embedded C, the hexadecimal number is written by 0x before the number. For example 55H is written as 0x55 and AAH is written as 0xAA.

Example 4.3 Write an 8051 C program to toggle all the bits of port P0 continuously.

Solution:

There can be two ways of writing this program:

(i) Using ~ inverter

```
#include <8051.h>
void main()
{
  while(1)                    //repeat continuously
  P0 = ~P0;                   // Toggle all the bits of port P0
}
```

Explanation: This program uses ~ inverter to toggle bits of port P0. It makes 0s as 1s and vice versa. while (1) is used to repeat the loop continuously.

(ii) Using data

```
#include <8051.h>
```

```
void main()
{
  while(1)                        //repeat continuously
      {
      P0 = 0x00;
      P0 = 0xFF;                  // Toggle all the bits of port P0
      }
}
```

Explanation: In this program, 00000000 is first sent to P0 by P0=0x00. Then 11111111 is sent to P0 by P0=0xFF. In this way, the data can be toggled. In this example, 00H and FFH are used, similarly any other data can be taken to show toggle operation.

Example 4.4 Write an 8051 C program to toggle all the bits of port P0 continuously with some delay.

Solution:

```
#include <8051.h>
void main()
{
unsigned int x;                  //declare a variable x
 for(;;)                         //repeat continuously
{
P0 = 0x55;
for(x=0;x<60000;x++);            //give some delay
P0 = 0xAA;                       // Toggle all the bits of port P0
for(x=0;x<60000;x++);            //give some delay
}
```

Explanation: In this program, a variable x has been taken using unsigned int. Then for giving delay, a for loop has been taken by initializing x as 0, incrementing it till x reaches 60000. the increment of x from 0 till 60000 takes some time and hence generates a delay. Note that since x takes value till 60000, unsigned int has to be used. The amount of delay can be varied by increasing or decreasing the limit of x. This type of delay is arbitrary and not accurate. In those applications, which require accurate value of time delay, timers should be used.

Example 4.5 Write an 8051 C program that reads input from a sensor connected to port P1, wait for some time and send it to LEDs connected to port P2.

Solution:

```
#include <8051.h>
void main()
{
P1=0xFF;                        //make P1 an input port
P2=0x00;                        //make P2 output port
unsigned char data_input;       //declare a variable x
while(1)                        // repeat continuously
{
data_input=P1;                  //get byte of data from P1        for(x=0;x<60000;x++);
        //give some delay
        P2= data_input;                 //send the data to P2
        for(x=0;x<60000;x++);           //give some delay
        }
        }
```

Explanation: Since in this program, real data is being used, the ports have been assigned input or output first. Port P1 has a sensor connected to it and data is incoming, hence it is made an input port by assigning 1s to all its bits by P1=0xFF. Similarly port P2 has LEDs connected to it and hence is made an output port by assigning 0s to all its bits by P2=0x00. Since the data cannot be sent directly from one port to another, a variable data_input is first declared by assigning unsigned char to it. The incoming data from sensor to P1 is sent to the variable data_input by data_input=P1. Then a delay is given by taking a for loop. The data from variable data_input is then sent to port P2 by P2= data_input and again some delay is given by using a for loop. The whole process is to be monitored continuously and hence, the whole process is kept in a while loop.

Example 4.6 Write an 8051 C program to turn P1.0 on and off continuously with some delay.

Solution:

```
#include <8051.h>
sbit LED = P1^0;                        // Using P1.0 as the LED pin
void main()
{
Unsigned int i;
LED=0;                                  //make bit P1^0 as output
while(1)
{
        LED = 1;                        // Turn on the LED
        for(i = 0; i < 50000; i++);     // Adding some delay
```

```
        LED = 0;                          // Turn off the LED
        for(i = 0; i < 50000; i++)        // Adding some delay
    }
    }
```

Explanation: In this program bit P1.0 is first declared outside the main program and assigned the name LED using sbit. In the main program, first the bit P1.0 is made an output bit as LED is connected to it. Then it is toggled by making it high first, giving some delay by for loop and again made low. The whole process is repeated continuously by keeping it in the while(1) loop.

Example 4.7 Write an 8051 C program to toggle P1.0 30000 times.

Solution:

```
#include <8051.h>
sbit LED = P1^0;                          // Using P1.0 as the LED pin
void main()
{
Unsigned int i;
LED=0;                                    //make bit P1^0 as output
for (i=0;i<30000;i++)
{
LED=1;
LED=0;
}
}
```

Explanation: Notice the difference between this program and the previous one. A simple sentence terminator i.e.; changes the whole operation of the program. Since here, a process is to be repeated 30000 times, the for loop is used as a counter. So the instructions in the for loop are repeated 30000 times. However, in the previous program, the for loop was followed by statement terminator. The for loop was used to generate a delay while the value of i reached a particular value.

Example 4.8 Write an 8051 C program to get a byte of data from P0 and send it to LEDs connected to P3. Use sfr data type.

Solution:

```
sfr P0 = 0x80;                            //declare P1 using sfr data type
sfr P3 = 0xB0;                            //declare P3 using sfr data type
void main(void)
{
        unsigned char this_byte
```

```
        P0=0xFF;                    //make P0 an input port
        P3=0x00;                    //make P3 an output port
        for(;;)                     //repeat continously
              {
              this_byte= P0;        //get data from P0
              P3= this_byte;        //send it to P3
              }
}
```

Explanation: This program does not start with a header file and makes use of sfr data type, which accesses RAM spaces of P0 and P2. In the main program, ports P0 and P3 are first made input and output ports by sending FFH and 00H respectively. A variable this_byte is declared using unsigned char this_byte, which gets the data from P0 using this_byte=P0. This data is then sent to P3 using P3= this_byte. An empty for loop for(;;) is used to repeat the process continuously as the data is coming repeatedly.

UNIT SUMMARY

In this chapter on Embedded C programming for the 8051 microcontroller, we delved into essential aspects crucial for programming within this embedded system. We commenced by exploring the fundamental data types utilized in 8051 C programming, crucial for understanding variable declarations and memory allocation. Subsequently, we scrutinized the syntax specific to Embedded C for the 8051, highlighting its nuances and conventions for effective programming. Lastly, we examined practical applications through a series of Embedded C programs tailored for the 8051, providing hands-on experience in implementing algorithms and functionalities within the constraints of this embedded environment. Through these discussions, readers gained a comprehensive understanding of how to leverage Embedded C to develop robust and efficient solutions for the 8051 microcontroller.

KNOW MORE

An interesting Story about development of microcontroller :

> John Harrison Wharton, the architect of 8051, was a junior engineer at Intel at the time the project to develop the 8051 was poised to kick off. He and his supervisor used to go out to lunch together on occasion. One day, they heard a rumor that there was going to be a lunchtime meeting about something or other and that free sandwiches were to be served, so they decided to slip in while no one was looking. While munching on the sandwiches, John listened to the various ideas that were being bounced around. Afterwards, he returned to his cubical and sketched out a block diagram of what would eventually form the architecture of the 8051.

EXERCISES

Multiple Choice Questions

4.1. The magnitude of unsigned char in C programming is?

(a) 0 to 255 (b) 0 to 128

(c) -128 to 127 (d) 0 to 450

4.2. To declare a variable of a person's age, which type of data should be used?

(a) Signed char (b) Signed int

(c) Unsigned char (d) Unsigned int

4.3. The signed int data type has how many bits?

(a) 8 bit (b) 4 bit

(c) 16 bit (d) 64 bit

4.4 What is the data range of the sbit data type?

(a) 0 to 255 (b) 0 to 62235

(c) SFR bit-addressable only (d) RAM bit-addressable only

4.5. The for loop is used in C programming for?

(a) Repeat continuously (b) Run one time only

(c) Run two times only (d) None of the above

4.6. The size of the hex file of C programming is_______ than assembly language?

(a) Smaller (b) Large

(c) Same (d) None of the above

4.7. In C programming the sbit should be declared ____?

(a) In void main (b) Outside of void main

(c) Both a and b (d) None of the above

4.8. How many different techniques are there in 8051 C programming to implement a time delay?

(a) 4 (b) 3

(c) 6 (d) 2

4.9. What type of file extension is used to load in a microcontroller to execute an instruction?

(a) .doc (b) .c

(c) .xlx (d) . hex

4.10. Which option is the right declaration if you want to continually toggle only bit P2.4 without interfering with the other bits of P2?

(a) sbit mybit = P2^4 (b) P2 = P2^1

(c) sbit mybit = P2^6 (d) P2 = P2^4

Answers of Multiple Choice Questions

4.1 (a), 4.2 (c), 4.3(c), 4.4 (c), 4.5 (a), 4.6 (a), 4.7 (b), 4.8 (d), 4.9 (d), 4.10 (a)

Short and Long Answer Type Questions

Short Answer Questions:

4.11 What is the advantage of programming a microcontroller in C?

4.12 Name various data types for 8051 C.

4.13 Which data types are most widely used in Embedded C programming for 8051?

4.14 Why is it important to learn data types for 8051 C?

4.15 Which data type should be used while measuring a room's temperature?

4.16 What is the difference between sbit and sfr data types?

Long Answer Questions:

4.17 Describe the role of a microcontroller in embedded systems and how C programming is utilized to control microcontroller behavior.

4.18 Write an 8051 C program to get data at bit P2.3 and send it to P1.7 continuously.

4.19 Write an 8051 C program to send a square wave of a few hundred hertz frequency at P3.4.

4.20 Write an 8051 C program to toggle bit P1.0 continuously using some delay. Use the sfr data type to declare bit address.

5

8051 Internal Peripherals and Related Programs

UNIT SPECIFICS

This unit elaborately discusses the following topics:

(i) Timers and Counters

(ii) Serial Communication

(iii) Interrupts

(iv) Power Saving Operation

At the chapter's conclusion, you'll find a variety of question formats, including multiple choice, short answer, and long answer. These questions are designed to deepen understanding, covering both basic and advanced concepts. Additionally, the chapter provides a list of suggested readings for further exploration. Students can also use QR codes placed throughout the chapter to access additional resources.

RATIONALE

Learning about the 8051's internal peripherals is important because it allows students to gain practical experience in programming and interfacing with hardware components like timers, counters, serial ports, and interrupt systems.. Knowledge of 8051 peripherals helps students understand the working of embedded systems, which are integral to many modern electronic devices.Working with 8051 peripherals requires students to solve real-world problems, enhancing their troubleshooting and analytical skills thus preparing them for careers in industries that utilize these systems.

PRE-REQUISITES

Familiarity with the general architecture of 8051 microcontroller and its Pin Diagram

UNIT OUTCOMES

After completing the unit, the students will be able to:

U5-O1: Learn to configure and use Timer 0 and Timer 1 for various timing and counting applications.

U5-O2: Understand the serial communication interface (UART) of the 8051.

U5-O3: Implement simple programs for serial data transmission and reception.

U5-O4: Configure and handle interrupts using the Interrupt Enable (IE) and Interrupt Priority (IP) registers.

Unit-5 Outcomes	EXPECTED MAPPING WITH COURSE OUTCOMES (1- Weak Correlation; 2- Medium correlation; 3- Strong Correlation)					
	CO-1	CO-2	CO-3	CO-4	CO-5	CO-6
U5-O1	3	-	1	-	-	-
U5-O2	3	1	-	-	-	-
U5-O3	3	2	-	2	-	-
U5-O4	3	2	1	-	-	1

5.1 Introduction to 8051 Internal Peripherals

The 8051 microcontroller comes with a set of on-chip peripherals that facilitate various functions by providing a wide range of capabilities, thereby making it a versatile microcontroller. These on-chip peripherals, more commonly known as internal peripherals, include timers/counters, which facilitate precise timing operations and event counting; serial communication interfaces, such as UART, that are essential for data exchange with other devices; and programmable I/O ports, which enable the microcontroller to interact with external world such as interfacing with sensors and actuators. Additionally, an interrupt system in 8051 allows it to respond promptly to external events, thereby improving real-time performance.

These built-in peripherals improve real-time performance, simplify circuit design by reducing the need for external components. Moreover, these peripherals are highly customizable, thereby making the 8051 an efficient choice for a wide range of applications, from simple automation tasks to complex control systems.

5.2 8051 Timers and Counters

Among the many features of 8051, the built-in timers and counters are crucial components that allow it to handle a wide range of timing and counting tasks, making it ideal for applications that require precise timing control, generating specific time delays and counting external events.

5.2.1 Introduction to 8051 Timers

The 8051 microcontroller typically includes two 16-bit timers/counters: Timer 0 and Timer 1. These timers can operate in several modes, each providing different functionalities required for various applications. As far as timer mode and counter mode is concerned, the only difference is the clock source for incrementing the timer registers. Before studying these in detail, it is important to understand the concept of 8051 clock as these timers/counters work on the clock frequency.

8051 Clock

Every Timer needs a clock source to work properly. In 8051, the frequency of the attached crystal is used as the main clock frequency source for the timer and is 1/12th of XTAL oscillator frequency as shown in Fig.5.1.

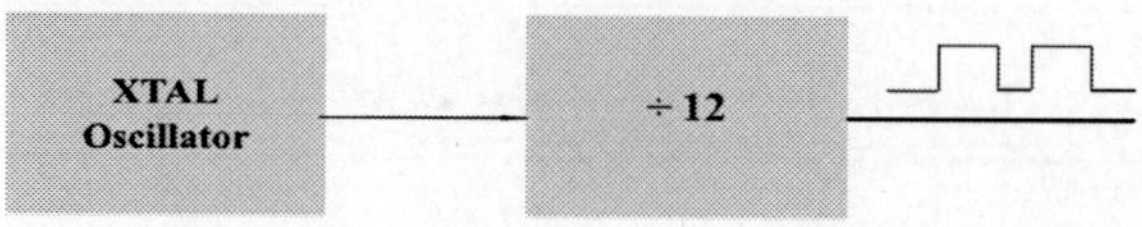

Fig.5.1 Clock Source for 8051 Timers

For example, if the frequency of the quartz crystal is 12 MHz, then the frequency for Timer will be 1/12 of crystal frequency i.e 1MHz . The time (T = 1/f) taken by the Timer to count by one is 1µs (1/1MHz). Similarly if an 11.0592 MHz crystal is used, the operating frequency of Timer is 921.6 KHz and the time period is 1.085 µs.

Timer/Counter 0

Timer 0 is a 16-bit timer/counter, meaning it can count from 0 to 65535. It is made up of two 8-bit registers: TL0 (Timer 0 Low byte) and TH0 (Timer 0 High byte), which can be combined to form a 16-bit timer/counter as shown in Fig.5.2.

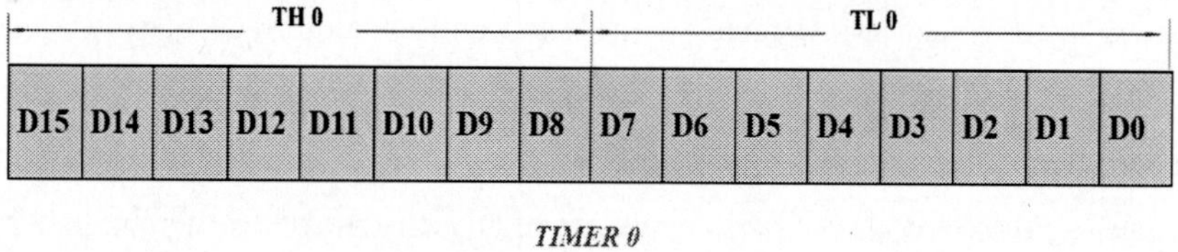

Fig. 5.2 Structure of Timer 0

TL0 (Timer 0 Low Byte)

TL0 is the lower 8-bit register of Timer 0, which stores the lower byte of the count value.

TH0 (Timer 0 High Byte)

TH0 is the upper 8-bit register of Timer 0, which stores the higher byte of the count value.

Timer/Counter 1

Timer 1, similar to Timer 0, is a 16-bit timer/counter and is made up of two 8-bit registers: TL1 (Timer 1 Low byte) and TH1 (Timer 1 High byte), which can be combined to form a 16-bit timer/counter as shown in Fig.5.3.

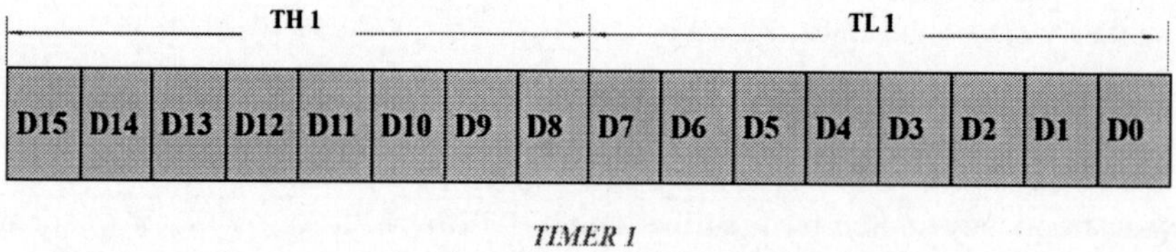

Fig 5.3 Structure of Timer 1

TL1 (Timer 1 Low Byte)

TL1 is the lower 8-bit register of Timer 1, which stores the lower byte of the count value.

TH1(Timer 1 High Byte)

TH1 is the upper 8-bit register of Timer 1, which stores the higher byte of the count value.

Timer Mode (TMOD) Register

Both Timers of 8051 can be configured in different modes, which will be studied in detail in coming subsections. TMOD register is an 8-bit register used to set these timer operation modes and hence, must be understood first. It is also used to decide if the operation of timers will be timer/counter. It is divided into two 4-bit fields: the upper 4 bits control Timer 1 and the lower 4 bits control Timer 0 as shown in Fig.5.4.

TMOD 7	TMOD 6	TMOD 5	TMOD 4	TMOD 3	TMOD 2	TMOD 1	TMOD 0
Gate	C/T	M1	M0	Gate	C/$\overline{T}$	M1	M0
Timer 1				Timer 0			

Fig.5.4 TMOD Register

For each timer, upper 2 bits are used to specify the operation while lower 2 bits are used to set the timer mode.

GATE

It is mainly used for gating control. Every timer needs a mechanism to start and stop. 8051 timers can be started or stopped by both hardware and software. By software means, they are controlled by the TR (timer start) bits-TR0 and TR1. Timers are started by using the instruction SETB TRx, where x=0 for Timer 0 and x=1 for Timer 1. Similarly both timers are stopped by instruction CLR TRx, where x=0 for Timer 0 and x=1 for Timer 1. In order to control the timers through software, GATE=0 in the TMOD register. Similarly timers can be controlled via external hardware source, GATE=1.

When GATE=0: Timer is enabled when TR0 (timer run control bit in TCON register) is set.

When GATE=1: Timer is enabled only while INT0 (external interrupt 0) is high and TR0 is set.

C/T It is mainly used to select timer/counter operation

When C/T =0, Timer mode is selected

When C/T =1, Counter mode is selected

M1 and MO

These are used to select the different operating modes of timers as shown in Table 5.1.

Table 5.1 Operating Modes using M1 and M0 bits

M1	M0	Mode	Operating Mode
0	0	0	13-bit timer mode
0	1	1	16-bit timer/counter mode

M1	M0	Mode	Operating Mode
1	0	2	8-bit Auto-Reload Mode
1	1	3	Split Timer Mode

Example 5.1 Find the value of TMOD register to operate the 8051 timer 1 in Mode 0 through software mode.

Solution: Let us first have a look at various bits of TMOD register

TMOD 7	TMOD 6	TMOD 5	TMOD 4	TMOD 3	TMOD 2	TMOD 1	TMOD 0
Gate	C/T	M1	M0	Gate	C/$\overline{T}$	M1	M0
Timer 1				Timer 0			

Since this program involves timer 1, all lower 4 bits of timer 0 are made 0. Similarly it is controlled through software, which means GATE=0. Next, Mode can be chosen by M1 and MO as shown in Table 5.1. As seen, both M1 and M0 are made 0 in order to choose Mode 0. Now, we can put these values in TMOD register as shown below:

TMOD 7	TMOD 6	TMOD 5	TMOD 4	TMOD 3	TMOD 2	TMOD 1	TMOD 0
Gate 0	C/$\overline{T}$ 0	M1 0	M0 0	Gate 0	C/$\overline{T}$ 0	M1 0	M0 0
Timer 1				Timer 0			

Hence TMOD is 00H.

Example 5.2 Find the value of TMOD register to operate the 8051 timer 0 in Mode 2 through software mode.

Solution: Let us first have a look at various bits of TMOD register

TMOD 7	TMOD 6	TMOD 5	TMOD 4	TMOD 3	TMOD 2	TMOD 1	TMOD 0
Gate	C/T	M1	M0	Gate	C/$\overline{T}$	M1	M0
Timer 1				Timer 0			

Since this program involves timer 0, all lower 4 bits of timer 1 are made 0. Similarly it is controlled through software, which means GATE=0. Next, Mode can be chosen by M1 and MO as shown in Table 5.1. As seen, M1=1 and M0=0 in order to choose Mode 2. Now, we can put these values in TMOD register as shown below:

TMOD 7	TMOD 6	TMOD 5	TMOD 4	TMOD 3	TMOD 2	TMOD 1	TMOD 0
Gate 0	C/$\overline{T}$ 0	M1 0	M0 0	Gate 0	C/$\overline{T}$ 0	M1 1	M0 0
Timer 1				Timer 0			

Hence TMOD = 00000010B

=02H

Operating Modes of Timers

The four operating modes of timers by different combinations of M1 and M) are as follows:

Mode 0 (13-bit Timer Mode): In this mode, the lower 5 bits of the TH0 register remain unused and hence, Timer 0 operates as a 13-bit timer. This mode is rarely used due to its limited 13-bit range.

Mode 1 (16-bit Timer Mode): This mode makes full use of both the TL0 (Timer Low byte) and TH0 (Timer High byte) registers, and hence Timer 0 operates as a 16-bit timer. It is the most commonly used mode for general timing applications.

Mode 2 (8-bit Auto-Reload Mode): In this mode, Timer 0 functions as an 8-bit timer with automatic reload. The TL0 register counts from 0 to 255, and upon reaching the maximum value, it is reloaded with the value in the TH0 register. This mode finds its applications in situations where precise time intervals are required.

Mode 3 (Split Timer Mode): As the name suggests, this mode splits Timer 0 into two 8-bit timers: TL0 and TH0. In this mode, there is additional flexibility as each 8-bit timer can be used as an independent 8-bit timer.

Among all 4 modes, Mode 1 is the most widely used and will be studied in detail in following subsection:

Mode 1 Programming

Let us understand how timers operate in Mode 1 in order to understand the functioning of timers. Timer 1 is a 16-bit timer and hence values from 0000 to FFFH can be loaded into the timer's registers TH and TL. For example, FFF0 will be loaded as FF in TH and F0 in TL as shown in Fig. 5.5.

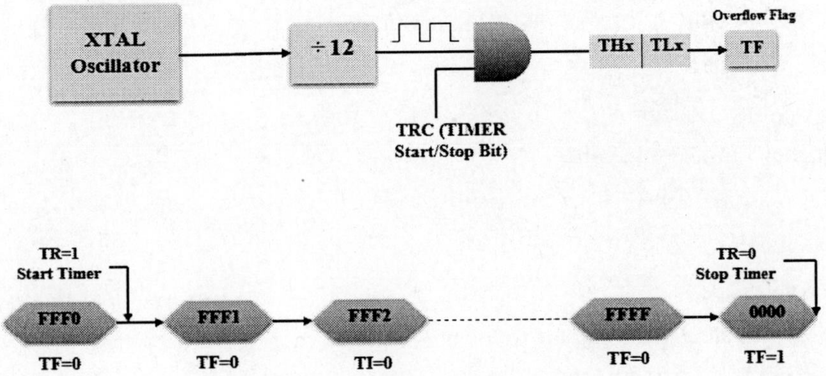

Fig. 5.5 Timer Operation in Mode1

After loading 16-bit initial values into TH and TL, the timer is started using TR (Timer Flag) using instruction SETB TR. On being started, it starts counting up from the value loaded i.e FFF0 until it reaches its limit of FFFFH. When it reaches its limit of FFFFH, it rolls over to 0000 and this sets high TF (timer flag) bit. TF is monitored continuously and when it becomes high, the timer is stopped by using instruction CLR TR. Also, TH and TL are reloaded with the original value, TF is reset to 0 and the process is repeated. It must be noted that for Timer 0, TL0, TH0, TF0 and TR1 will be used while for Timer 0, TL0,TH0, TF0 and TR1 will be used.

Time Delay Calculations When using Timer in Mode 1

Timers are used to generate accurate time delays and hence it is important to calculate the time delay generated. As discussed earlier, timer works with a clock frequency of 1/12th of Crystal frequency($F_{crystal}$). Therefore, $f=1/12\ F_{crystal}$

The time period of each clock can be calculated as T=1/f. Suppose AABB is the Hex value to be loaded into the timer. Then AA will be loaded into TH and BB will be loaded into TL respectively. Then delay will be calculated by following formula:

$$(FFFF-AABB+1) * T$$

FFFF-AABB gives the number of counts required for counting from AABB till FFFF. Since there is a rollover from FFFF to 0000 at the end of timer operation, 1 additional count is accounted for and added in the formula.

Example 5.3 Calculate the delay generated by Timer 1 using Model in the following code. Assume that the crystal oscillator runs at 12 MHz frequency.

```
        MOV TMOD, #10H      ; Timer 1, mode 1(16-bit mode)
        MOV TL1,#DFH        ;Place the lower byte of count in TL1
        MOV TH1,#61H        ;Place upper byte of count in TH1
        SETB TR1            ; Start timer
WAIT:   JNB   TF1, WAIT     ; wait till TF1 becomes high
        CLR TR1             ; Stop timer
        CLR TF1             ; Clear timer flag bit
```

Solution:

Crystal frequency ($F_{crystal}$) = 12 Mhz,

$f=1/12\ F_{crystal}$

f= 1/12 * 12 = 1 MHz,

Therefore, T= 1/f = 1μs.

Time Delay can be calculated using the following formula:

Time Delay= (FFFF-AABB +1) * T

Total Number of counts = (FFFF- 61DF)+1

= 65536 - 45535 +1

= 20000

Therefore, Time Delay = 20000 *1 μs = 20ms.

5.3 Serial Communication

5.3.1 Introduction to Serial Communication

Serial Communication refers to the process of sending data sequentially one bit at a time over a communication bus. It is mainly used for long-distance communication between two systems located at distances ranging from hundreds of feet to millions of miles apart. This reduces the number of electrical connections thus, simplifying wiring.

There are two ways of Serial communication namely Synchronous and Asynchronous data communication. Synchronous Data Communication sends blocks of data at a time along with a clock signal to keep the sender and receiver synchronized while asynchronous data communication sends one byte at a time. It manages both data transmission and reception asynchronously, meaning it doesn't require a clock signal to synchronize the data and mainly relies on start and stop bits to signify the beginning and end of data packets. Examples of Serial communication are SPI (Serial Peripheral Interface) and I2C (Inter-Integrated Circuit) while that of Asynchronous data communication is RS-232. It is tedious to write long programs for these communications and hence, there are special chips manufactured for serial communication known as UART (universal asynchronous receiver / transmitter) and USART (universal synchronous asynchronous receiver / transmitter). The 8051 microcontroller has a built-in UART that allows it to communicate with other serial devices. Hence, we will study this in more detail in coming subsections.

5.3.2 8051 Serial Communication

For serial communication with 8051, the COM port of IBM PC/compatible computers is mainly used. In order to understand data transfer between the PC and 8051 based system, it should be ensured that the baud rate of the 8051 system matches the baud rate of the PC's COM port.

Baud Rate

Baud rate is the rate at which data is transmitted, measured in bits per second (bps). Common baud rates include 9600, 14400, 19200, and 115200 bps. The baud rate in 8051 is programmable using Timer 1 in 8-bit auto-reload mode. The 8051's UART divides the machine cycle frequency by 32 before it is used by Timer 1 for setting the baud rate.

Assuming Crystal frequency ($F_{crystal}$) = 11.0592 MHz, Machine Cycle frequency is 11.0592/12 = 921.6 kHz. This is further divided by 32 to give 28,800 Hz, which is used to find the Timer 1 value to set the baud rate as shown in Fig.5.6.

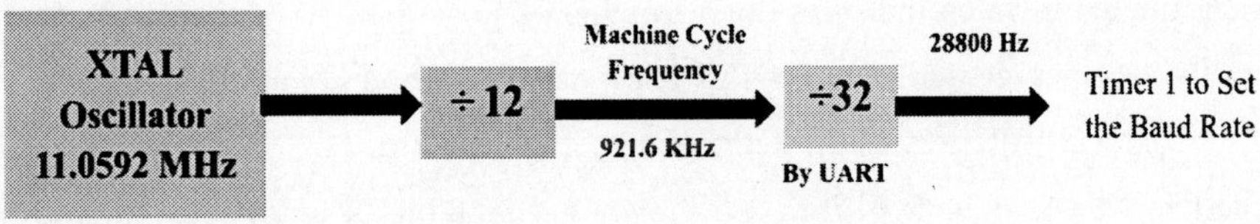

Fig.5.6 UART Frequency to Set Baud Rate

In order to get baud rates compatible with the PC, the TH1 in Timer 1 must be loaded with values, which can be calculated using Table 5.2.

Table 5.2 Timer TH1 Value for Different Baud Rates

(Assuming Crystal frequency($F_{crystal}$) = 11.0592 MHz)

BAUD RATE	TH1 (DECIMAL)	TH1 (HEX)
1200	-24	FD
2400	-12	F4
4800	-6	FA
9600	-3	FD

Data Framing in Asynchronous Serial Communication

In a serial transmission, the data received at the receiving end of the data line is in the form of 0s and 1s, which makes it difficult to interpret. Hence, it is desirable to form a set of rules called a protocol, which is agreed by both sender and receiver so that both the sender and receiver can properly interpret the data. This protocol determines how the data is packed, how many bits make a character and when does the data begin and end. In asynchronous serial communication, bits of data are organised into a predefined format where each character is placed between start and stop bit. This format is known as data framing as shown in Fig.5.7.

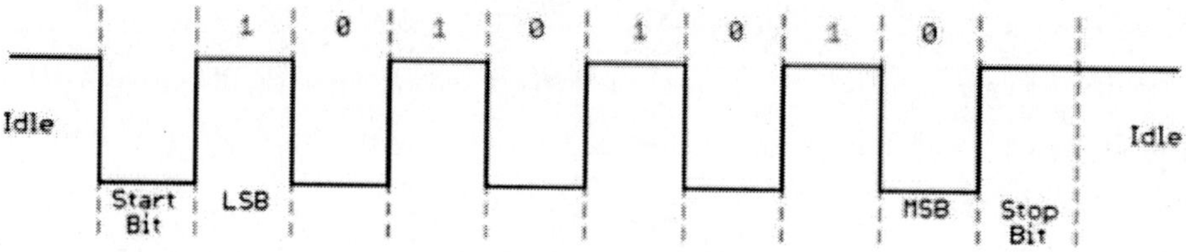

Fig.5.7 Data Framing in UART Serial Communication

In asynchronous serial communication, each frame typically consists of:

1. Start Bit
2. Data Transfer Bits
3. Parity Bit (optional)
4. Stop Bits

The start bit is a single bit which indicates the beginning of a data packet and is usually set low (logic 0). It mainly helps the receiver recognize the start of a new data frame and synchronize with the incoming data package. Data Transfer Bits Represent the actual data being transmitted and hold the information intended for communication. These can be 5, 6, 7, 8, or 9 bits long, with 8 bits (1 byte) being the most common.

Parity bit is used to detect single-bit errors in the data bits. It is optional and provides a simple form of error checking.

Stop Bit indicates the end of a data packet and is usually set high (logic 1). It provides a brief pause to allow the receiver to process the received byte and prepare for the next one.

These bits in data framing can be programmed using a special function register (SFR) known as SCON (Serial Control) register. This is discussed in the following subsection.

Serial Port Configuration (SCON Register)

The 8051 has a special function register (SFR) called SCON (Serial Control) to configure the serial port. It is an 8-bit register used to program the bits in start bit, data bits and stop bit of data framing and is shown in Fig. 5.8.

Fig. 5.8 SCON Serial Port Control Register

SCON Register							
SCON.7	SCON.6	SCON.5	SCON.4	SCON.3	SCON.2	SCON.1	SCON.0
SM0	SM1	SM2	REN	TB8	RB8	T1	R1

SM0 (SCON.7) Serial mode bit 0

SM1 (SCON.6) Serial mode bit1

SM2 (SCON.5) Enables multiprocessor communication (usually set to 0)

REN (SCON.4) Receiver enable (set to 1 to enable serial reception)

TB8 (SCON.3) Not widely used

RB8 (SCON.2) Not widely used

T1 (SCON.1) Transmit Interrupt flag. It is automatically set when the last bit of one byte is sent.

R1(SCON.0) Receive interrupt flag. It is automatically set when reception is complete SM0 and SM1 take different combinations to give four serial communication modes as shown in Table 5.3.

Table 5.3. Serial Communication Modes

SM0	SM1	Serial Communication Mode	Description
0	0	Mode 0	8-bit shift register (synchronous)
0	1	Mode 1	8-bit UART (asynchronous) variable baud rate
1	0	Mode 2	9-bit UART (asynchronous) fixed baud rate
1	1	Mode 3	9-bit UART (asynchronous) variable baud rate

Out of the four serial communication modes, Mode 1 is most widely used as it allows variable baud rate set by Timer 1 of the 8051 microcontroller. Moreover, in this mode, the data framing is composed of 8 bits, 1 stop bit and 1 start bit, making it compatible with the COM port of IBM./compatible PCs.

SBUF Register

SBUF is an 8 bit register which is crucial for serial communication. It acts as the primary data buffer for the UART (Universal Asynchronous Receiver/Transmitter) system, allowing for data transmission and reception. The byte of data is placed in the SBUF register when transmitted through the TxD line. Similarly, it is placed in the SBUF register when received through the RxD line. When a byte of data is written into SBUF register, 8051 frames it with start and stop bits and then it is transferred serially through the TxD pin. Similarly, when received through the RxD line, 8051 deframes it by eliminating start and stop bits and then placed in the SBUF register.

Steps for Programming 8051 for Transmission Data Serially

While programming 8051 for transferring data serially, the following steps are followed:

1. Load SCON with 50H, to select the 8-bit , 1-Start and 1-Stop bit mode
2. Load the Timer1 with 20H to configure it for auto reload mode(Mode-2)
3. Load the baud rate generator value to TH1 to set the baud rate
4. Set TR1 to 1 to start the Timer for baud rate generation
5. Load the new char to be transmitted into SBUF.
6. Wait till the char is transmitted. TI will be set when the data in SBUF is transmitted.
7. Clear the TI for the next cycle.
8. Go back to Step 5 to transfer the next character

Example 5.4 Write an assembly language program to transmit "A" serially at 9600 baud rate using 8051 microcontroller. Assume 11.0592 MHz clock.

Solution:

```
        ORG 00H                 ; Origin at 00H address
        MOV SCON, #50H ; Serial mode 1, 8-bit data, 1 stop bit, REN enabled
        MOV TMOD, #20H          ; Timer 1 in mode 2
        MOV TH1, #0FDH          ; Load TH1 to set baud rate to 9600
        SETB TR1                ; Start Timer 1
AGAIN:MOV SBUF, #'A'            ; Load the the serial buffer register with 'A'
WAIT: JNB TI, WAIT              ; Wait for the transmission to complete
        CLR TI                  ; Clear the TI bit
        SJMP AGAIN              ; Go back to transfer the next character
```

Steps for Programming 8051 for Receiving Data Serially

While programming 8051 for receiving data serially, the following steps are followed:

1. Load SCON with 50H, to select the 8-bit , 1-Start and 1-Stop bit mode
2. Load the Timer1 with 20H to configure it for auto reload mode(Mode-2)
3. Load the baud rate generator value to TH1 to set the baud rate
4. Set TR1 to 1 to start the Timer for baud rate generation
5. Clear RI flag for data reception
6. Wait till the char is received. RI will be set when the data in SBUF is received.
7. Move contents data from SBUF to desired location
8. Go back to Step 5 to receive the next character

Example 5.4 Write an assembly language program to receive data serially at 9600 baud rate using 8051 microcontroller and store it in RAM location 40H. Assume 11.0592 MHz clock.

Solution:

```
ORG 00H                 ; Origin at 00H address
MOV SCON, #50H          ; Serial mode 1, 8-bit data, 1 stop bit, REN enabled
MOV TMOD, #20H          ; Timer 1 in mode 2
MOV TH1, #0FDH          ; Load TH1 to set baud rate to 9600
SETB TR1                ; Start Timer 1
AGAIN: CLR RI           ; Clear RI for receiving data
WAIT: JNB RI, WAIT      ; Wait for the character
MOV A, SBUF             ; Save data of SBUF into accumulator
MOV 40H, A              ; Store data in RAM location 40H
SJMP AGAIN              ; Go back to transfer the next character
```

5.4 Interrupts

5.4.1 Introduction to Interrupts

In many real-time processes, in order to execute an external event, the actual task must be temporarily halted for some time. It performs the required action and then returns to the main task to resume the main task. In such scenarios, 8051 features a very powerful mechanism known as interrupts. Interrupts in the 8051 microcontroller are mechanisms that temporarily suspend the main program execution to service an external event or perform a specific task, then pass the control to the main program and resume from where it had left off. It is very different from the polling method wherein the microcontroller continuously checks the status of each device sequentially, performs the service if the status condition is met and then moves to the next device.It keeps monitoring sequentially until each device is serviced. Polling is not an efficient use of microcontroller as it consumes more processor time.

Differences between Interrupts and Polling

(i) In interrupts, the microcontroller can serve many devices at a time based on priority assigned to them. However, since in the polling method, the microcontroller checks the status of each device sequentially, it cannot assign priority to them.

(ii) In the interrupt method, the microcontroller can ignore a device for service, while this is not possible in the polling method.

(iii) Interrupt method saves time of microcontroller and is more preferred over polling method, which wastes time of processor by polling devices which do not require service.

Due to various advantages of the interrupt method, it is widely used and most preferred for microcontroller applications requiring execution of an external event.

5.4.2 Interrupts in 8051

The 8051 microcontroller supports five sources of interrupts, each associated with specific functionalities. These are as follows:

1. Two External Interrupts (INT0 and INT1)

These interrupts are triggered by external pins on the microcontroller (P3.2 and P3.3). These are also sometimes called EX1 and EX2. They can be configured to be level-triggered or edge-triggered.

2. Two Timer Interrupts (TF0 and TF1)

Two interrupts are kept aside for the timers-Timer 0 and Timer 1. These interrupts are generated by the overflow of Timer 0 and Timer 1.

3. One Serial Communication Interrupt (RI/TI)

There is a single interrupt in serial communication for both receive (RI) and transmit (TI). This interrupt is triggered by the serial port when a byte has been received (RI) or transmitted (TI).

In many manufacturers' data sheets, there are six interrupts as they include reset also as an interrupt. As discussed in previous chapters, during power -up reset,the 8051 jumps to 0000 address when the reset pin is activated.

Interrupt Service Routine (ISR)

For every interrupt, an interrupt handler or Interrupt Service Routine (ISR) is there which is run every time the interrupt is invoked. When an interrupt occurs, ISR comes into the picture, which instructs the processor to take appropriate action for the interrupt. After ISR execution, the controller jumps to the main program and resumes from where it had left off.

Interrupt Vector Table

For each interrupt, a certain number of bytes are set aside for each interrupt and there is a fixed location in memory which holds the address of its ISR. The interrupt vector table in the 8051 microcontroller assigns specific memory locations to each interrupt as shown in Table 5.4.

Table 5.4 Interrupt Vector Table for 8051

Interrupt Type	ROM Locations (HEX)	PIN
External Interrupt 0 (INT0)	0x0003	P3.2
Timer 0 Overflow (TF0)	0x000B	
External Interrupt 1 (INT1)	0x0013	P3.3
Timer 1 Overflow (TF1)	0x001B	
Serial Port Interrupt (RI/TI)	0x0023	

Enabling and Prioritizing Interrupts

The 8051 microcontroller allows the user to enable and prioritize interrupts using Special Function Registers (SFRs) Interrupt Enable (IE) Register and Interrupt Priority (IP) register respectively. These are discussed below:

Interrupt Enable (IE) Register

When the reset pin is activated, all interrupts are disabled, which means that the microcontroller will not respond to them if they are activated. They must be enabled using software using the Interrupt Enable (IE) register. The IE register is an 8-bit register used to enable or disable interrupts. It is a bit-addressable register and each bit in this register corresponds to a specific interrupt as shown in Fig. 5.9.

D7	D6	D5	D4	D3	D2	D1	D0
IE.7	IE.6	IE.5	IE.74	IE.3	IE.2	IE.1	IE.0
EA	—	—	ES	ET1	EX1	ET0	EX0

Fig. 5.9. Interrupt Enable (IE) Register

EA Global Interrupt Enable/Disable.

If EA=0, it disables all interrupts and no interrupt will be acknowledged. If EA=1, each interrupt is individually enabled or disabled

— Reserved for future use

— Reserved for future use

ES Enable(1)/Disable(0) Serial Port Interrupt

ET1 Enable(1)/Disable(0) Timer 1 Overflow Interrupt

EX1 Enable(1)/Disable(0) External Interrupt 1

ET0 Enable(1)/Disable(0) Timer 0 Overflow Interrupt

EX0 Enable(1)/Disable(0) External Interrupt 0

Example 5.5 Write the instruction to enable global interrupt, serial interrupt, external interrupt 0, and Timer 0 interrupt

Solution:

MOV IE, #10000111B ; enable global interrupt,serial interrupt,external interrupt 0, Timer 0 interrupt

Interrupt Priority (IP) Register

In 8051, it is possible to assign priority levels to the interrupts by changing the corresponding bit in the Interrupt Priority (IP) register. There are certain rules to be kept in mind for priority interruptions, depending upon the level of priority:

1. If requests from two interrupts of different priority levels are received simultaneously, the higher priority level will be preferred over the low-priority interrupt.
2. High-priority interrupts can interrupt the execution of low-priority interrupt service routines and not vice versa. Also, a low priority interrupt cannot be interrupted by another low priority interrupt.
3. If requests from two interrupts of the same levels are received simultaneously, the internal polling sequence will determine which request is to be received.

Interrupt Priority is an 8-bit bit-addressable register and each bit in this register can be used to change the priority level of interrupts as shown in Fig. 5.10.

D7	D6	D5	D4	D3	D2	D1	D0
IP.7	IP.6	IP.5	IP.74	IP.3	IP.2	IP.1	IP.0
—	—	PT2	PS	PT1	PX1	PT0	PX0

Fig. 5.10. Interrupt Priority (IP) Register

—	Reserved for future use
—	Reserved for future use
PT2	serial port interrupt priority level.
PS	serial port interrupt priority level
PT1	timer interrupt of 1 priority
PX1	external interrupt priority level
PT0	timer0 interrupt priority level
PX0	external interrupt of 0 priority level

5.5 Power Saving Operation

There are many applications in Embedded systems, where power consumption is the main constraint. In these situations, power down and Idle mode are inbuilt power-saving features in 8051, which are used to save power. There are mainly two power-saving modes in 8051 microcontroller:

- Power Down Mode
- Idle Mode

Let us now understand the differences between power down mode and Idle mode.

Difference Between Power Down & Idle Mode

In Power Down mode, the peripheral clock and CPU remain inactive since the oscillator clock provided to the system is inactive.

In Idle Mode, only the clock provided to the CPU gets deactivated, whereas the peripherals clock will remain active in this mode.

Hence power saved in power-down mode is more than in idle mode.

The main differences between Power Down & Idle Mode are shown in table Table 5.5.

Table 5.5 Difference Between Power Down & Idle Mode

Power Saving Mode	Peripheral Clock	CPU	Power Saved
Power Down	Inactive	Inactive	More
Idle Mode	Active	Inactive	Lesser

PCON Register: Power control register

8051 has a power control register (PCON) for power control. Let's see the power control register.

PCON (Power Control) is an 8-bit register in 8051 for power control, which forces the 8051 microcontrollers to go to power-saving mode It contains two power-saving mode bits (PD, IDL) and one serial baud rate control bit (SMOD) as shown in Fig.5.10.

PCON.7	PCON.6	PCON.5	PCON.4	PCON.3	PCON.2	PCON.1	PCON.0
SMOD	—	—	—	GF1	GF0	PD	IDL

Fig.5.11. PCON (Power Control) Register

The function of each bit is explained in Table 5.5.

Table 5.5. PCON (Power Control) Register

Bit	Symbol	Description
PCON.7	SMOD	Serial Communication Baud Rate Modify Bit **1**= Baud rate is doubled in UART mode 1,2 and 3. **0**= No effect on Baud rate
PCON.6-PCON.4	—	—
PCON.3	GF1	General Purpose User Flag (Bit 1)

Bit	Symbol	Description
PCON.2	GF0	General Purpose User Flag (Bit 0)
PCON.1	PD	Power Down Bit 1= Enable Power-Down mode 0= Disable Power-Down mode
PCON.0	IDL	Idle Mode Bit 1= Enable Idle mode 0= Disable Idle mode

PCON register can be programmed just like a general purpose register. Let us see some examples to understand the programming of PCON for entering different modes.

Example 5.5 Write the instruction to enter idle mode using the PCON register.

Solution:

PCON.7	PCON.6	PCON.5	PCON.4	PCON.3	PCON.2	PCON.1	PCON.0
SMOD	—	—	—	GF1	GF0	PD	IDL
0	0	0	0	0	0	0	1

MOV PCON, #01H ; Set IDL bit to enter Idle mode

Example 5.6 Write the instruction to enter power-down mode using the PCON register.

Solution:

PCON.7	PCON.6	PCON.5	PCON.4	PCON.3	PCON.2	PCON.1	PCON.0
SMOD	—	—	—	GF1	GF0	PD	IDL
0	0	0	0	0	0	1	0

MOV PCON, #02H ; Set PD bit to enter Power-down mode

Example 5.6 Write the instruction to doubling the baud rate using (i) SMOD bit (ii) PCON register.

Solution:

(i) Using SMOD register

PCON.7	PCON.6	PCON.5	PCON.4	PCON.3	PCON.2	PCON.1	PCON.0
SMOD	—	—	—	GF1	GF0	PD	IDL
1	0	0	0	0	0	0	0

SETB SMOD ; Set SMOD bit to double the baud rate

(ii) Using PCON register:

PCON.7	PCON.6	PCON.5	PCON.4	PCON.3	PCON.2	PCON.1	PCON.0
SMOD	—	—	—	GF1	GF0	PD	IDL

1	0	0	0	0	0	0	0

MOV PCON, 80H; Set SMOD bit in PCON register to double the baud rate

UNIT SUMMARY

This unit covers essential features of the 8051 microcontroller, focusing on its timers and counters, serial communication, interrupts, and power-saving operations. First subsection explains the configuration and usage of the 8051's timers and counters, highlighting their role in timing operations and event counting. Serial communication explains the usage of the 8051's timers and counters, highlighting their role in timing operations and event counting. Then the unit introduces the concept of interrupts, explaining how the 8051 handles external and internal events efficiently. Finally, the unit discusses various power-saving modes available in the 8051, such as idle and power-down modes, which are crucial for energy-efficient designs.

KNOW MORE

SCAN THESE QR CODES TO LEARN MORE ABOUT 8051 TIMERS

EXERCISES

Multiple Choice Questions

5.1. Which of the following registers is used to control the operation of timers in the 8051 microcontroller?

a) TCON
b) PCON
c) SCON
d) TMOD

5.2. What is the function of the TCON register in the 8051 microcontroller?

a) Controls the mode of timers

b) Controls the start/stop and overflow of timers

c) Configures the serial communication mode

d) Controls the power mode of the microcontroller

5.3. How many timers are available in the standard 8051 microcontroller?

a) 1 b) 2

c) 3 d) 4

5.4. What is the size of each timer register (TH0, TL0, TH1, TL1) in the 8051 microcontroller?

a) 8 bits b) 16 bits

c) 4 bits d) 32 bits

5.5. What is the maximum delay that can be generated using Timer 0 in Mode 1 (16-bit timer mode) of the 8051 microcontroller if the clock frequency is 12 MHz?

a) 65536 μs b) 65536 ms

c) 65.536 ms d) 1.048576 s

5.6. In which mode does the 8051 timer act as a 13-bit timer?

a) Mode 0 b) Mode 1

c) Mode 2 d) Mode 3

5.7. Which bit in the TCON register is used to start or stop Timer 0 in the 8051 microcontroller?

a) TR1 b) TF0

c) TR0 d) TF1

5.8. What happens when a timer in the 8051 microcontroller overflows?

a) The microcontroller resets b) The overflow flag is set

c) The timer stops automatically d) The timer continues without any change

5.9. Which mode of the 8051 timer is also known as the auto-reload mode?

a) Mode 0 b) Mode 1

c) Mode 2 d) Mode 3

5.10. If Timer 1 is set to Mode 2, what will happen when the timer overflows?

a) The microcontroller will reset

b) The timer will stop

c) The timer will reload a value from TH1 and continue counting

d) The timer will switch to Mode 1

5.11 What is the typical baud rate used for serial communication in the 8051 microcontroller?

a) 9600 b) 2400

c) 4800 d) 19200

5.12. Which register is used to control the mode of serial communication in the 8051 microcontroller?

a) SCON b) TCON

c) PCON d) TMOD

5.13. In the 8051, which bit in the SCON register is used to enable reception of data?

a) TI b) RI

c) SM0 d) REN

5.14. What is the function of the TI flag in the SCON register of the 8051 microcontroller?

a) Indicates data transmission is complete b) Enables transmission of data

c) Enables reception of data d) Indicates data reception is complete

5.15. What is the role of the SM0 and SM1 bits in the SCON register?

a) They control the baud rate

b) They select the serial communication mode

c) They enable the serial communication

d) They reset the serial port

5.16. Which of the following is the correct combination of serial communication modes supported by the 8051 microcontroller?

a) Mode 0, Mode 1, Mode 2, Mode 3
b) Mode 1, Mode 2, Mode 3, Mode 4

c) Mode 0, Mode 1, Mode 3, Mode 4
d) Mode 0, Mode 2, Mode 3, Mode 4

5.17. In the 8051 microcontroller, which timer is typically used to set the baud rate for serial communication?

a) Timer 0
b) Timer 1

c) Timer 2
d) Timer 3

5.18. Which register holds the data to be transmitted or received via serial communication in the 8051?

a) SBUF
b) SCON

c) PCON
d) TCON

5.19. What is the function of the SMOD bit in the PCON register?

a) Enables double baud rate
b) Disables serial communication

c) Enables reception mode
d) Resets the microcontroller

5.20. In 8051 serial communication, which of the following modes allows for 9-bit data transmission?

a) Mode 0
b) Mode 1

c) Mode 2
d) Mode 3

5.21. How many interrupt sources are available in the 8051 microcontroller?

a) 3
b) 4

c) 5
d) 6

5.22. Which interrupt has the highest priority in the 8051 microcontroller?

a) Timer 0
b) External Interrupt 0 (INT0)

c) Serial Communication
d) External Interrupt 1 (INT1)

5.23. What is the vector address for the Timer 1 interrupt in the 8051 microcontroller?

a) 0003H
b) 000BH

c) 0013H
d) 001BH

5.24. Which register is used to enable or disable specific interrupts in the 8051 microcontroller?

a) TCON
b) IE

c) IP
d) SCON

5.25. In the 8051, what is the function of the IP register?

a) Sets the interrupt vector addresses
b) Enables or disables interrupts

c) Sets the priority level of interrupts
d) Holds the interrupt flags

5.26. Which bit in the IE register is used to globally enable or disable all interrupts?

a) EA
b) ET0
c) EX0
d) ES

5.27. What happens if two interrupts occur at the same time in the 8051 microcontroller?

a) The interrupt with the higher priority is serviced first.
b) The interrupt with the lower priority is serviced first.
c) Both interrupts are ignored.
d) The microcontroller resets.

5.28. Which interrupt is associated with the serial communication in the 8051 microcontroller?

A) INT0
B) INT1
C) TF0
D) RI/TI

5.29. The external interrupts INT0 and INT1 in the 8051 microcontroller can be triggered by which of the following?

a) Level-triggered only
b) Edge-triggered only
c) Both level-triggered and edge-triggered
d) Timer overflow

5.30. In the 8051 microcontroller, how is the interrupt priority defined when both IE and IP registers are used?

a) IE sets the priority and IP enables the interrupts.
b) IP sets the priority and IE enables the interrupts.
c) Both IE and IP set the priority.
d) Both IE and IP enable the interrupts.

5.31. What is the primary purpose of the PCON register in the 8051 microcontroller?

a) To control the serial communication
b) To manage power modes and control the baud rate
c) To set the priority of interrupts
d) To configure the I/O ports

5.32. Which bit in the PCON register is used to double the baud rate of serial communication?

a) IDL
b) PD
c) SMOD
d) GF1

5.33. What happens when the PD (Power Down) bit in the PCON register is set to 1?

a) The microcontroller enters idle mode.
b) The microcontroller stops all operations and consumes minimal power.
c) The microcontroller doubles the baud rate.
d) The microcontroller resets.

5.34. Which of the following bits in the PCON register puts the 8051 microcontroller into idle mode?

a) SMOD
b) PD
c) IDL
d) GF0

5.35. What are the general-purpose flag bits (GF1 and GF0) in the PCON register used for?

a) They are used to indicate the status of power modes.

b) They are user-defined bits for general-purpose applications.

c) They control the baud rate of serial communication.

d) They enable or disable the microcontroller interrupts.

Answers of Multiple Choice Questions

5.1 (d) , 5.2 (b), 5.3 (b), 5.4 (a), 5.5 (c), 5.6 (a), 5.7 (c), 5.8 (b), 5.9 (c), 5.10 (c),5.11 (a) , 5.12 (a), 5.13 (d), 5.14 (a), 5.15 (b), 5.16 (a), 5.17 (b), 5.18 (a), 5.19 (a), 5.20 (c) , 5.21 (c) , 5.22 (b), 5.23 (c), 5.24 (b), 5.25 (c), 5.26 (a), 5.27 (a), 5.28 (d), 5.29 (c), 5.30 (b), 5.31 (b),5.32 (c), 5.33 (b),5.34 (c),5.35 (b)

Short and Long Answer Type Questions

Short Answer Questions:

5.36 What are the primary functions of the timers in the 8051 microcontroller?

5.37 Explain the difference between Timer Mode 1 and Timer Mode 2 in the 8051.

5.38 How is the Timer 0 of the 8051 configured for counter mode operation?

5.39 What role does the TCON register play in the operation of timers and counters in the 8051?

5.40 Describe how to generate a time delay using Timer 1 in the 8051 microcontroller.

5.41 How can you use the 8051 timers to measure the frequency of an external signal?

5.42 What is the significance of the gate control bit (GATE) in timer operations?

5.43 Describe the process of setting up Timer 0 in Mode 3 in the 8051 microcontroller.

5.44 What is the purpose of the TH and TL registers in the 8051 timers?

5.45 How does the overflow flag (TF) function in the 8051 timer operation?

5.46 What is the purpose of the SCON register in the 8051 microcontroller?

5.47 Explain the function of the SM0 and SM1 bits in the 8051 microcontroller.

5.48 How is the baud rate calculated in the 8051 microcontroller?

5.49 Describe the role of the SBUF register in serial communication.

5.50 What is the significance of the TI and RI flags in the 8051?

5.51 How can you enable serial communication in the 8051 microcontroller?

5.52 What are the different modes of serial communication supported by the 8051?

5.53 How does the SMOD bit in the PCON register affect serial communication?

5.54 What is the function of the REN bit in the SCON register?

5.54 Explain how interrupts are used in serial communication in the 8051 microcontroller.

5.55 How many interrupt sources are available in the 8051 microcontroller? List them.

5.56 What is the purpose of the IE (Interrupt Enable) register in the 8051?

5.57 Describe the function of the IP (Interrupt Priority) register in the 8051 microcontroller.

5.58 Explain the difference between level-triggered and edge-triggered external interrupts in the 8051.

5.59 What is the vector address for the External Interrupt 1 (INT1) in the 8051?

5.60 How does the 8051 microcontroller handle multiple simultaneous interrupts?

5.61 What happens when the EA (Enable All Interrupts) bit in the IE register is cleared?

5.62 Describe the role of the RI (Receive Interrupt) and TI (Transmit Interrupt) flags in serial communication.

5.63 How can the 8051 microcontroller be programmed to change the priority of an interrupt?

5.64 What is the function of the TF0 and TF1 flags in the context of timer interrupts in the 8051?

5.65 What is the function of the SMOD bit in the PCON register of the 8051 microcontroller?

5.66 Explain the role of the PD (Power Down) bit in the PCON register.

5.67 How does setting the IDL bit in the PCON register affect the 8051 microcontroller?

5.68 Describe the purpose of the general-purpose flag bits GF0 and GF1 in the PCON register.

5.69 What are the differences between the Power Down mode and Idle mode in the 8051 microcontroller as controlled by the PCON register?

5.70 How can the PCON register be used to optimize power consumption in the 8051 microcontroller?

5.71 In what scenario would you use the Power Down mode controlled by the PCON register?

5.72 How does the PCON register influence the serial communication baud rate in the 8051 microcontroller?

5.73 Can the 8051 microcontroller be woken up from Power Down mode? If so, how?

5.74 Why might a designer choose to use the Idle mode over the Power Down mode in a low-power application?

6 Software Development Tools

UNIT SPECIFICS

This unit elaborately discusses the following topics:

- Software Development Tools
- Keil Compiler
- Flash Magic

The questions at the back of chapter are mainly a large number of multiple choice questions as well as questions of short and long answer types. In order to inspire a deeper understanding among students, both lower and higher order of Bloom's taxonomy have been used to frame the questions. Some QR codes have also been provided in different sections which can be scanned for relevant supportive knowledge.

RATIONALE

Learning 8051 microcontroller programming using Keil compilers is essential for understanding the fundamentals of embedded systems development. Keil compilers provide a user-friendly environment for writing, compiling, and debugging code, making it easier for beginners to grasp core concepts of microcontroller programming.

PRE-REQUISITES

Knowledge of Assembly Language/ Embedded C Programming of 8051

UNIT OUTCOMES

After completing the unit, the students will be able to:

U6-O1: Understand various software development tools for 8051

U6-O2: Apply Keil Compiler in creating Hex file

U6-O3: Understand Flash Magic for burning Hex file into programmer

U6-O4: Create projects using Hex file and Flash Magic

Unit-6 Outcomes	EXPECTED MAPPING WITH COURSE OUTCOMES (1- Weak Correlation; 2- Medium correlation; 3- Strong Correlation)					
	CO-1	CO-2	CO-3	CO-4	CO-5	CO-6
U6-O1	3	-	1	-	-	-
U6-O2	3	1	-	-	-	-
U6-O3	3	2	-	2	-	-
U6-O4	3	2	1	-	-	1

6.1 Software Development Tools of 8051

As discussed in the previous chapter, the various programming languages of 8051 can be broadly categorized as:

- Machine Language
- Assembly Language
- High Level Language

We have already discussed the assembly language, various instruction sets related to development of programs based on assembly language as well as Embedded C for 8051. While developing the code for microcontrollers, the programmers make use of assembly language or high level language. Personal computers are used to develop and edit the programs for the targeted microcontroller. Various softwares such as assembler, debugger, compiler, simulator etc are then used to convert the program written in assembly language/high level language into machine language. A development system known as integrated development environment, comprising of development processor (personal computer), software and target controller, is used to program the microcontroller. In the following sections, we will mainly concentrate on Keil compiler, a software development tool for 8051 in detail.

6.2 Introduction to Keil Software

Keil, a Germany based Software development company has developed a cross compiler by the same name Keil. It provides several development tools like:

- Integrated Development environment (IDE)
- Project Manager
- Simulator
- Debugger
- C-Cross Compiler , Cross Assembler, Locator/Linker

Before starting working with the Keil software, one has to be well familiar with the concepts of compilers and cross compilers. They have been discussed in the following paragraphs:

6.2.1 Compilers

Compiler is a program that translates source code into object code. the way It works by looking at the entire piece of source code, collecting them and reorganizing the instruction and thus derives its name from its entire performance. Many compilers are available for the same language, each being unique for different computers.

- **Cross compiler**

  Cross compiler is a type of compiler that when run on one type of computer produces the object code for a different type of computer. It is similar to the compilers but the program is written for the target processor (like 8051 and its derivatives) on the host processors. An embedded platform having limitations such as no provision of any hard disk, restricted RAM provision and limited I/O capabilities, needs a fast host machine such as PC for editing and compiling the codes and downloading the resulting executable codes to the target to be tested. This is achieved by the use of the cross compilers. Cross compilers are helpful whenever the host machine has more resources such as memory, disk capability, I/O etc as compared to the target. Keil C Compiler is one such compiler that supports a huge number of host and target combinations. It supports as a target the 8 bit microcontrollers like Atmel and Motorola etc.

- **Advantages of Cross compiler**

  A cross compiler has the following advantages:

  - Its speed is very fast.
  - It has improved reliability.
  - Its maintenance is comparatively easy.
  - It does not need the knowledge of the processor instruction set.
  - Its register allocation and addressing mode details are managed by the compiler itself.
  - It provides improvement in the program readability.
  - C compilers are available for almost all target systems as C language is very portable and popular. Existing software investments can quickly and easily be converted from or adapted to other processors or environments

6.3 Keil Software Development Tools

There are several software development tools provided by the Keil Software for the use of 8051 family of microcontrollers. One can generate embedded applications for the multitude of 8051 derivatives by making use of such tools. Keil provides the following tools for 8051 development:

i. C 51 Optimizing C Cross Compiler,

ii. A 51 Macro Assembler,

iii. 8051 Utilities (linker, object file converter, library manager),

iv. Source-Level Debugger/Simulator,

v. µVision for Windows Integrated Development Environment.

The three main tools included in the Keil 8051 tool kit are: assembler, compiler and linker. All these are described here.

6.3.1 Assembler

An assembler is used to assemble the 8051 assembly program. In other words, it can be said that the assembler is employed to convert the assembly language program into a machine language program. It is essentially required since the microcontroller understands only in terms of binary numbers.

6.3.2 Compiler

A compiler is used to compile the C source-code into an object file. This has already been discussed in section 3.2.

6.3.3 Linker

A linker is used to create an absolute object module suitable for the in-circuit emulator. An absolute object file or module contains no relocatable code or data. All the code and data reside at fixed memory locations. The absolute object file may be used to perform the following functions:

- Programming of a Flash ROM or other memory devices.
- Simulation and target debugging.
- Program testing.

6.4 Project Development Steps in 8051

Development of 8051 project needs the following steps to be taken:

- Creation of a project.
- Selection of the target chip from the device data-base.
- Configuration of the tool settings.
- Creation of source files in C or assembly language.
- Compilation or assembly of source files depending upon whether the program is written in C or assembly language.
- Building the application with the project manager.
- Linking the object files from compiler and assembler.
- Correction of errors in source files.
- Testing the linked application.

The above mentioned steps are almost like those for any other software development project. Detailed discussions of these steps are provided in the following section:

6.5 Use of Keil software

Following activities are needed to be performed for developing an 8051 project using Keil compiler:

6.5.1 Starting µVision

Click on the start menu to open Keil software, then program and then select the version of Keil (depending upon the version which is installed). Also µVision can be started by clicking on the following icon:

Window shown in Fig.6.1 will appear on the screen.

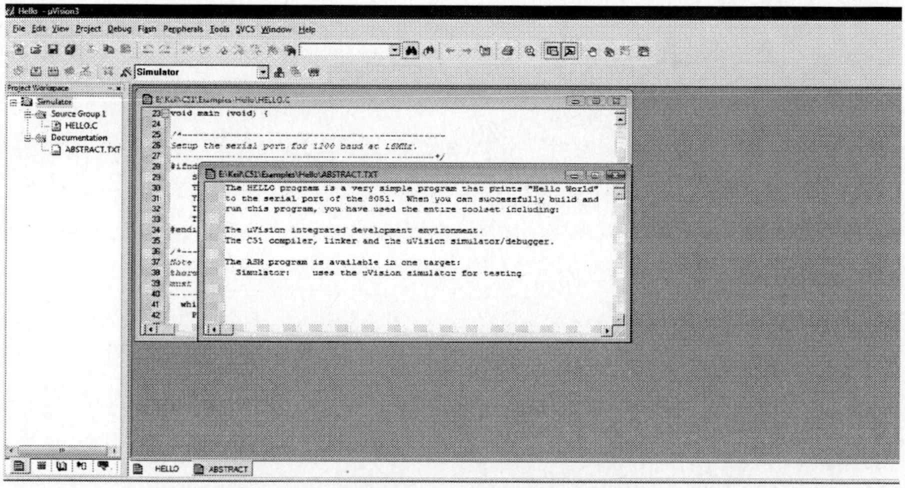

Fig.6.1 Window to start IDE of Keil

As observed from Fig.6.1, there are three different windows in this screen. These are:

- **Project work space window:** This is for showing all the related files connected with your project.
- **Editing window:** This is the place where the code can be edited.
- **Output window:** This shows the output when the project is compiled or built.

6.5.2 Creating a Project File

To create a new project file select from the µVision menu **Project** and then from the pull-down window, select **New Project** as shown in Fig.6.2.

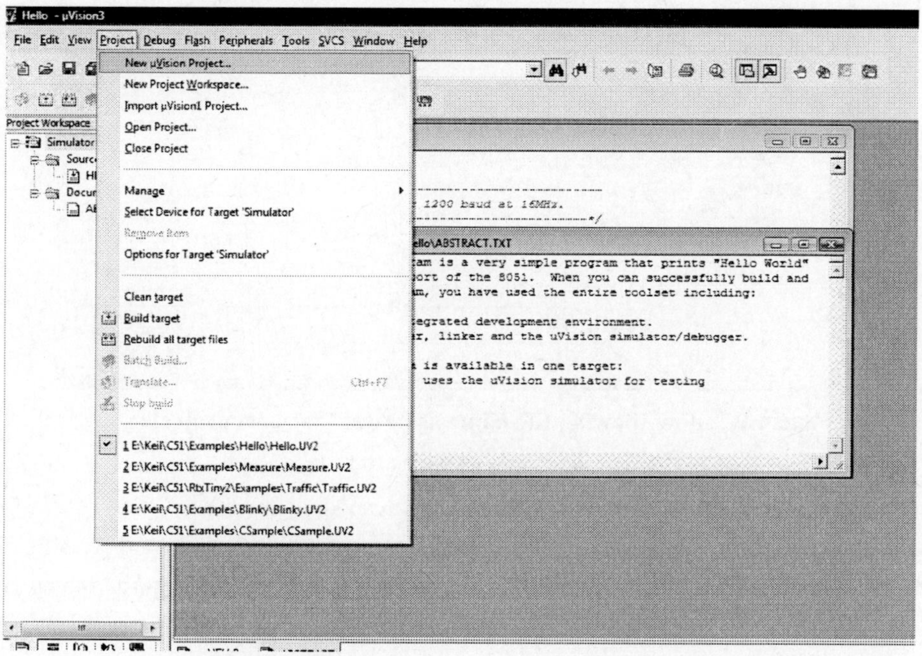

Fig.6.2 Window to create a new project

This will open a standard Windows dialog that asks for the new project file name, as shown in Fig.6.3.

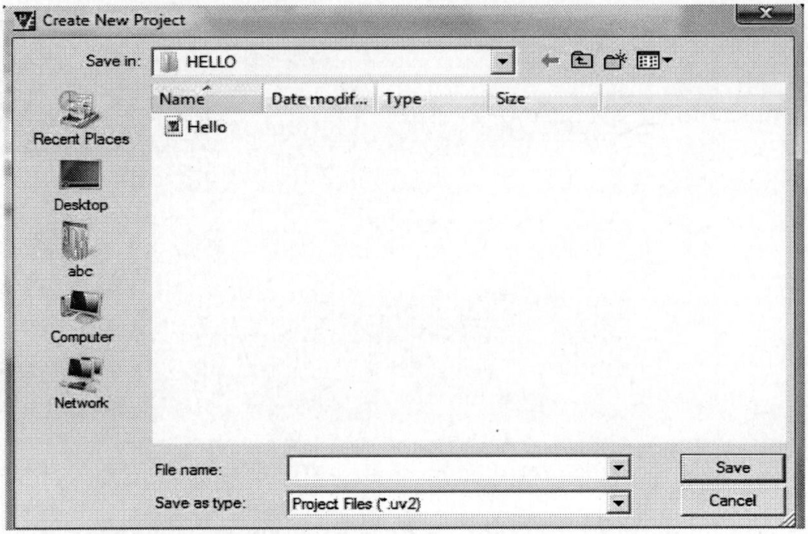

Fig.6.3 Window asking for new project's name

Enter the file name for the new project; let us say "First" as shown in Fig.6.4.

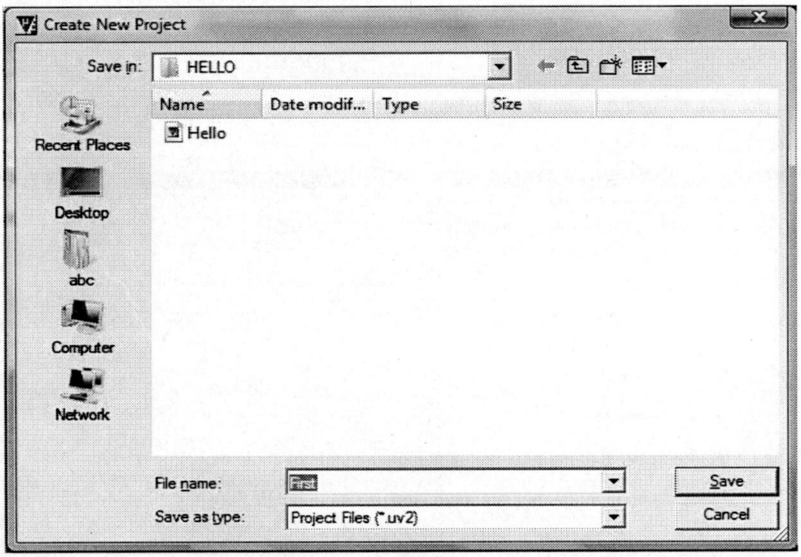

Fig.6.4 Window showing file name as "First" for new project

µVision3 creates a new project file with the name **FIRST.UV2** which will contain a default target and file group name. By default it will be saved as *.v2extension (depending upon the version of µVision).

Now it will ask to choose the target device for which one wants to write the program. Scroll down the cursor and select generic from the list. Expand the list and select 8051 (all variants) as shown in Fig.6.5.

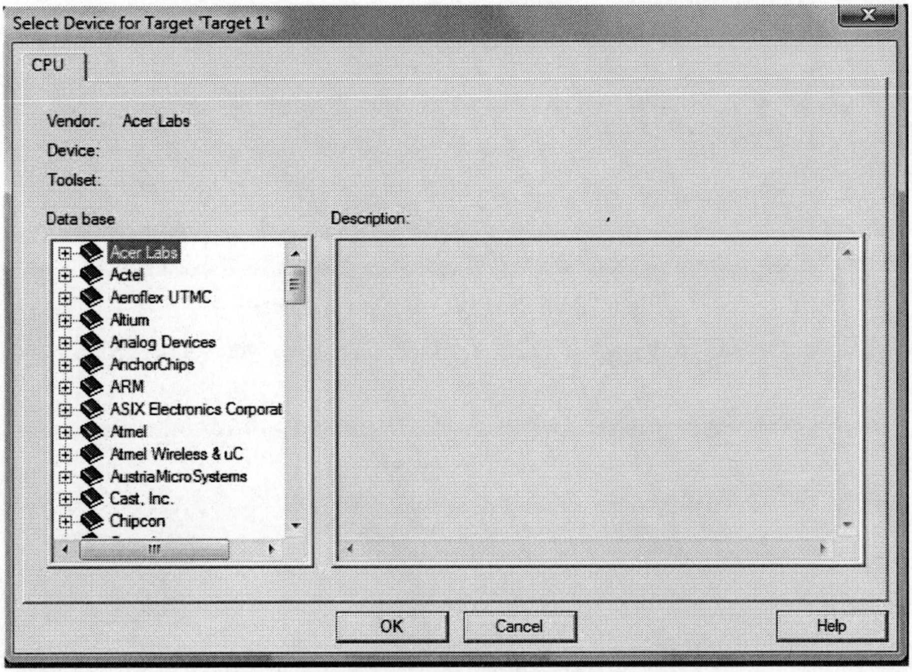

Fig.6.5 Window to select device for the project

Depending upon the type of microcontroller being used for the development of the project, choose the controller from the list provided. Let us take an example that P8xC51RD+ is used in the project, so accordingly it is selected as shown in Fig. 6.6.

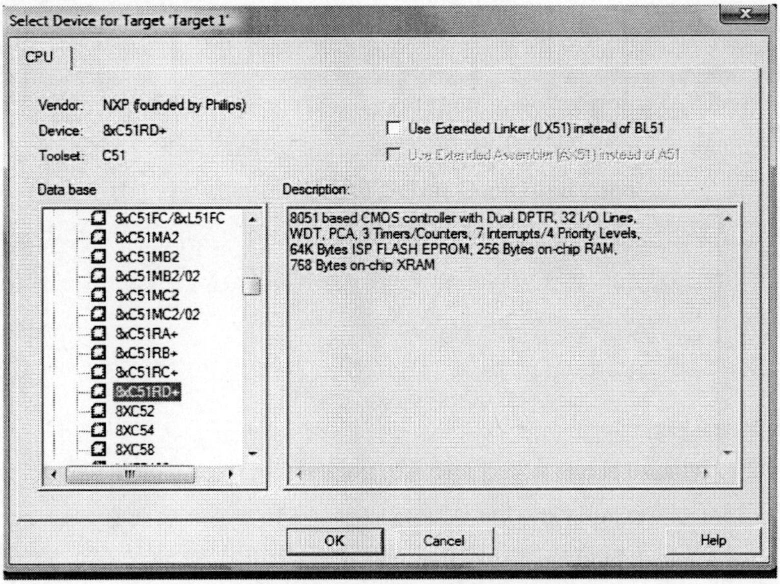

Fig.6.6 Window to select device

When OK is clicked, it will be asked to add startup code and file to the project folder as shown in Fig.6.7.

Fig.6.7 Window showing start up code

As can be seen in the project workspace in Fig. 6.8, a target is created with source group 1 and startup.a51 added to it.

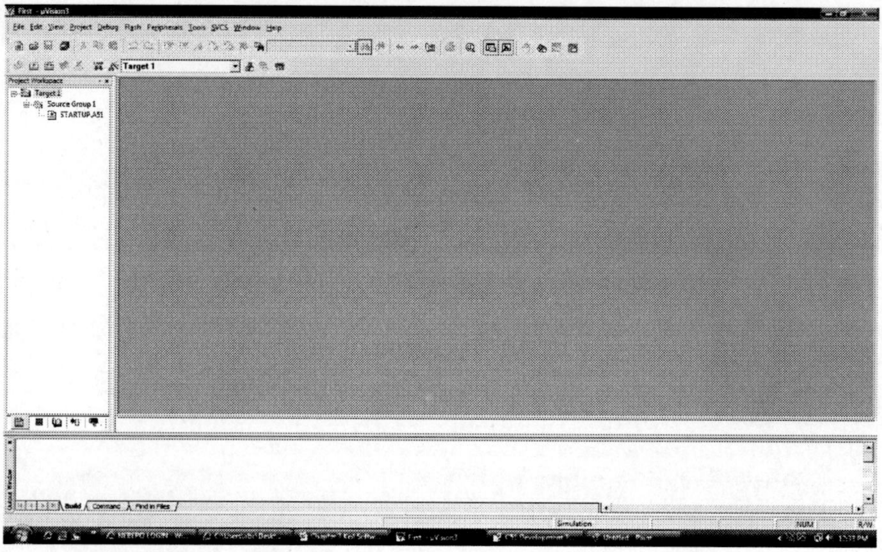

Fig.6.8 Window showing target created in project workspace

Now click on the file menu and select a new file. The editor window will open as shown in Fig.6.9. This window is used to write the code.

Fig.6.9 Editor window to write the code

Similar to C, a header file has to be included first. Since the target controller is 8051, the header file will be "reg51.h. A right click on the file (after the header file has bee included) will give an option 'open document <reg51.h>'. On selecting this option, the window shown in Fig.6.10 will appear.

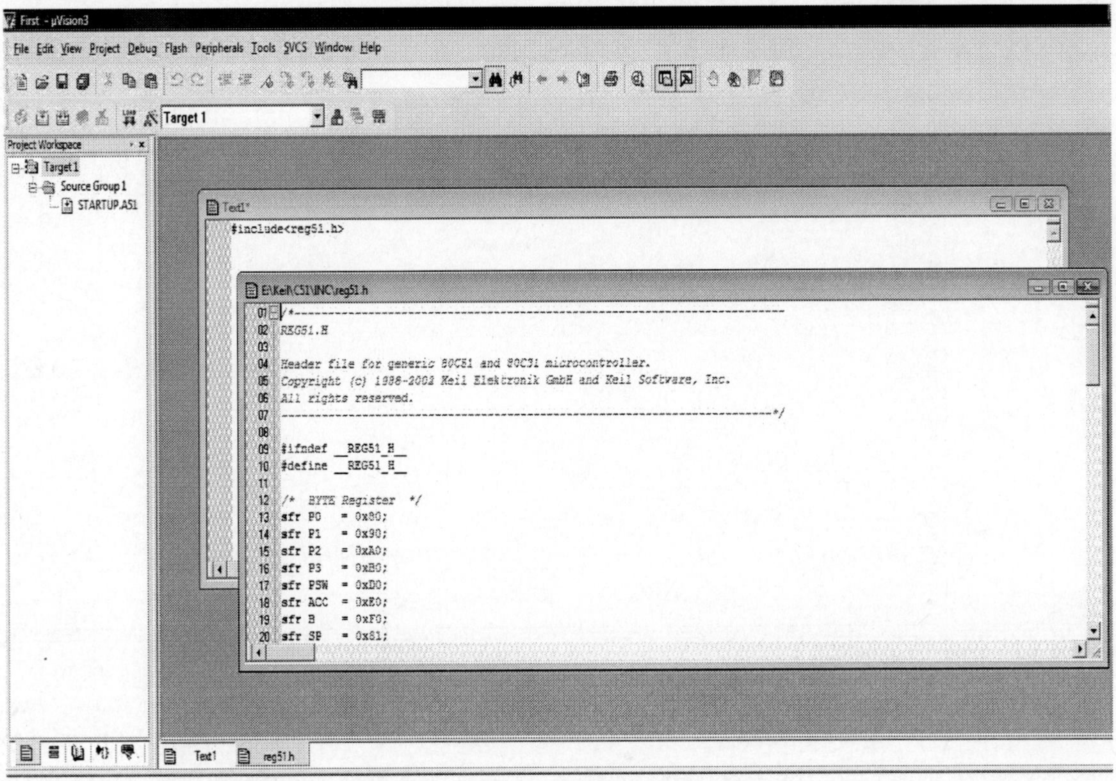

Fig.6.10 Window showing header file

One can see that all the Special Function Registers (SFRs) such as P0-P3, TCON, TMOD, ACC, bit registers and byte registers are already defined in this header file. Hence, one can directly use these register names in the program.

Now write the program code in C and save the file in project folder with ".c" extension. A program written in assembly language may be saved with ".asm" extension. An example showing a program written in C is shown in Fig.6.11.

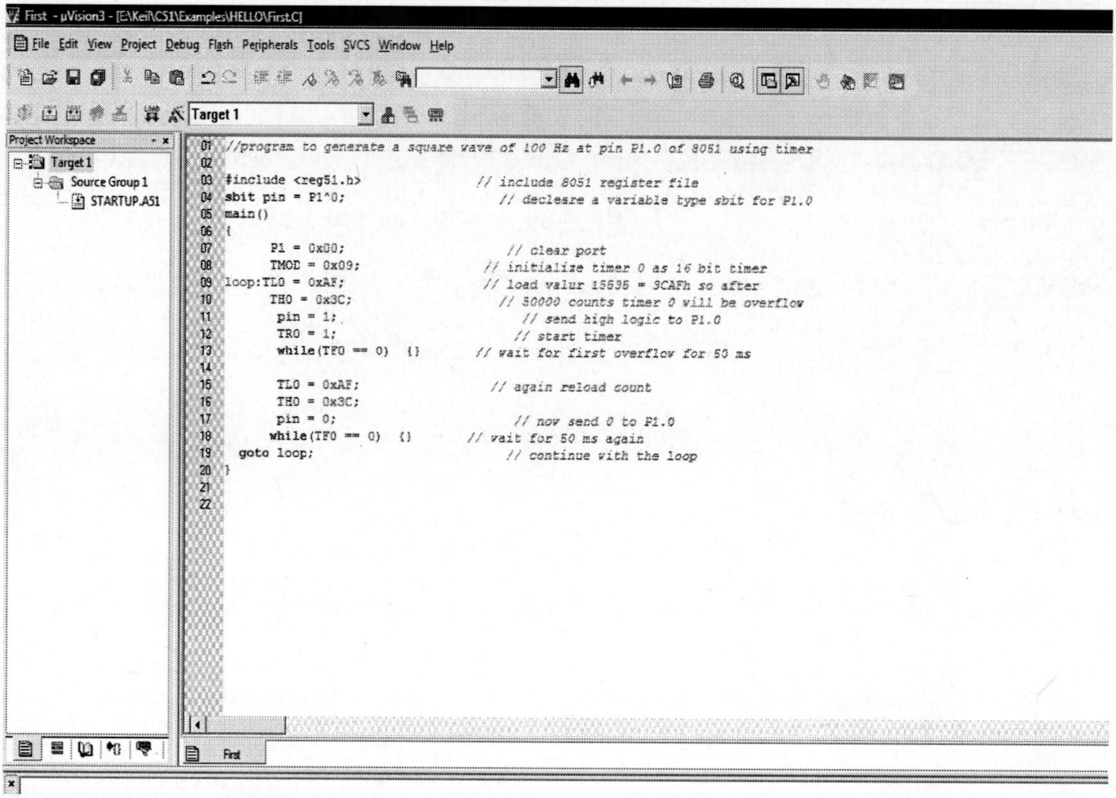

Fig.6.11 Window showing program written in C

As can be observed from Fig.6.11, the program is stored as *"First.C"* and the whole path of location of program is also shown. Once the program is saved, it is to be added to the source group1 created in project workspace. This is done by right clicking on "source group 1" in project workspace window and selecting "add files to source group 1" as shown in Fig.6.12.

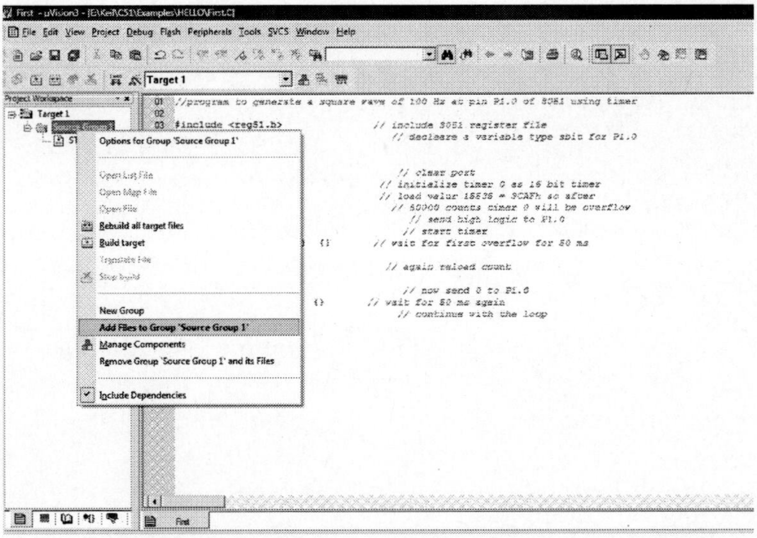

Fig.6.12 Adding program files to Group 'Source Group1'

This will open another window showing all created program files in the selected folder as shown in Fig.6.13. By default, it will show the program files saved in .C extension.

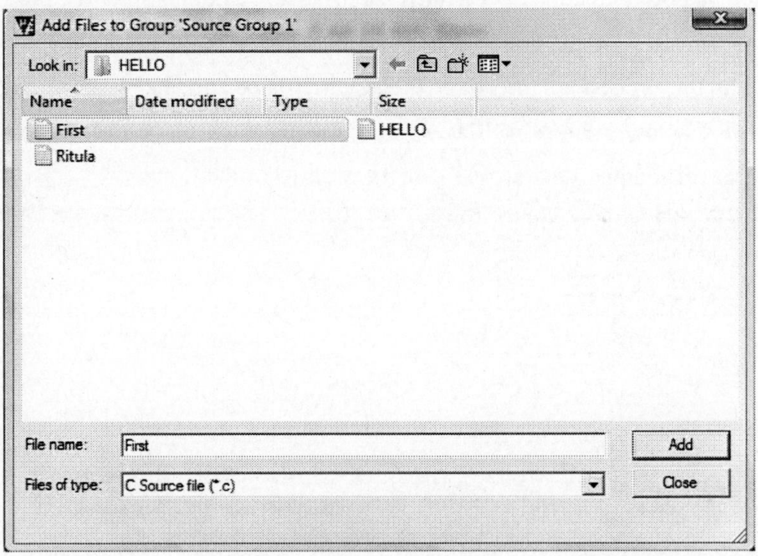

Fig.6.13 Window showing program files created in C

In case, program is written in assembly language and saved with .asm extension, one will have to change "Files of type" option shown in Fig.6.13. Since in this case, the program file was saved in .C extension, select the C file created as "First.C" and click add button.

One can see that the C file has been added in source group as shown in Fig.6.14.

Fig.6.14 Program File "First.C" added in Source Group1

6.5.3 Building Project

Once a project file has been created successfully, the next task is to compile the program by building a project. To build a project, go to the project menu and then select "build target" to compile the program as shown in Fig.6.15. In this process, all the source files are translated and linked. If a program contains syntax errors, µVision will display errors as well as warning messages in the output window. Also in case the program is error free, the output window will give the message of "0 Error(s)".

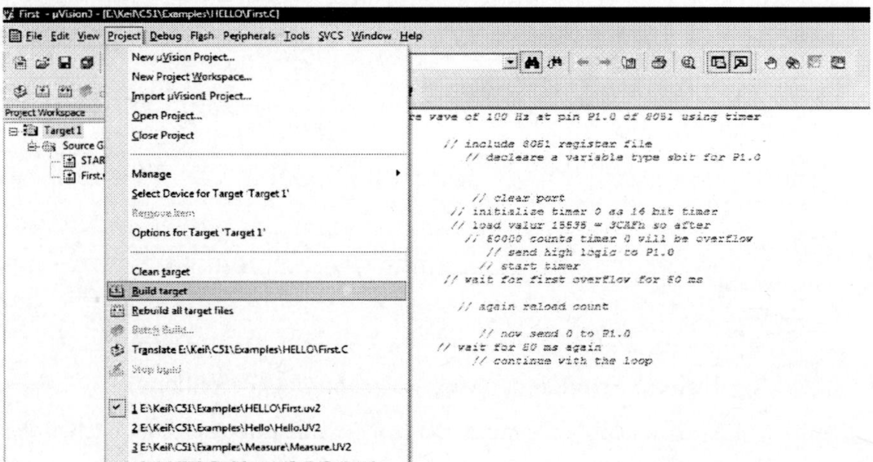

Fig.6.15 Window showing how to compile program

This can also be done by selecting the toolbar icon .

The output window will show the progress as shown in Fig.6.16.

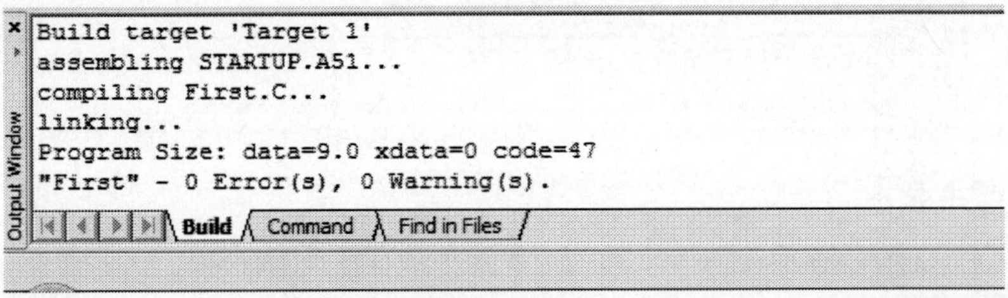

Fig.6.16 Output Window Showing Messages After Compiling the Program

In case there are compilation errors in the program, the target will not be created. All the errors have to be removed and again the target shall be built till the output window shows "0 Error(s)". Now it may be assumed that the project building stage is complete.

6.5.4 Running the Program

Now the program is ready for run. Select the Start/ Stop session from the debug menu as shown in Fig.6.17.

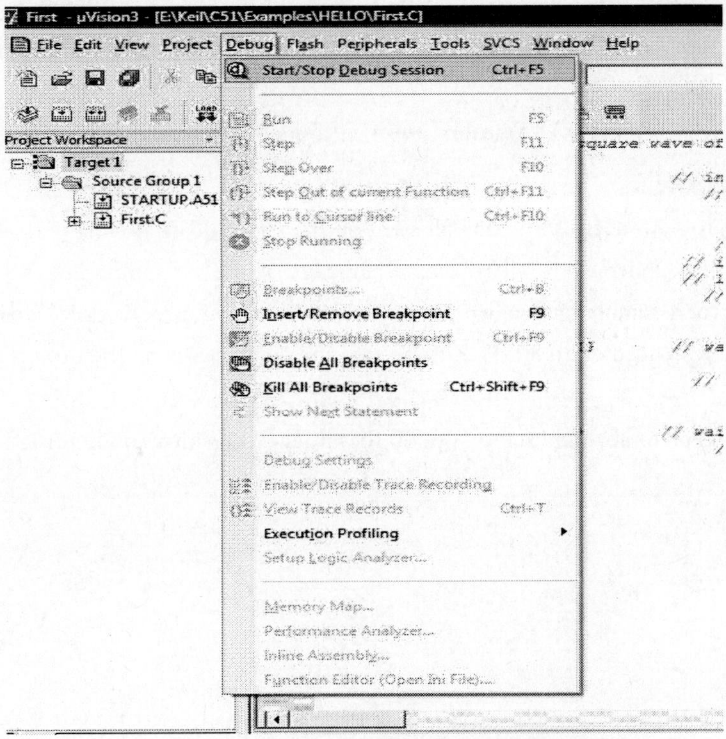

Fig.6.17 Window showing start/Stop Debug Session

The window shown in Fig.6.18 will appear after the Start/Stop session is selected.

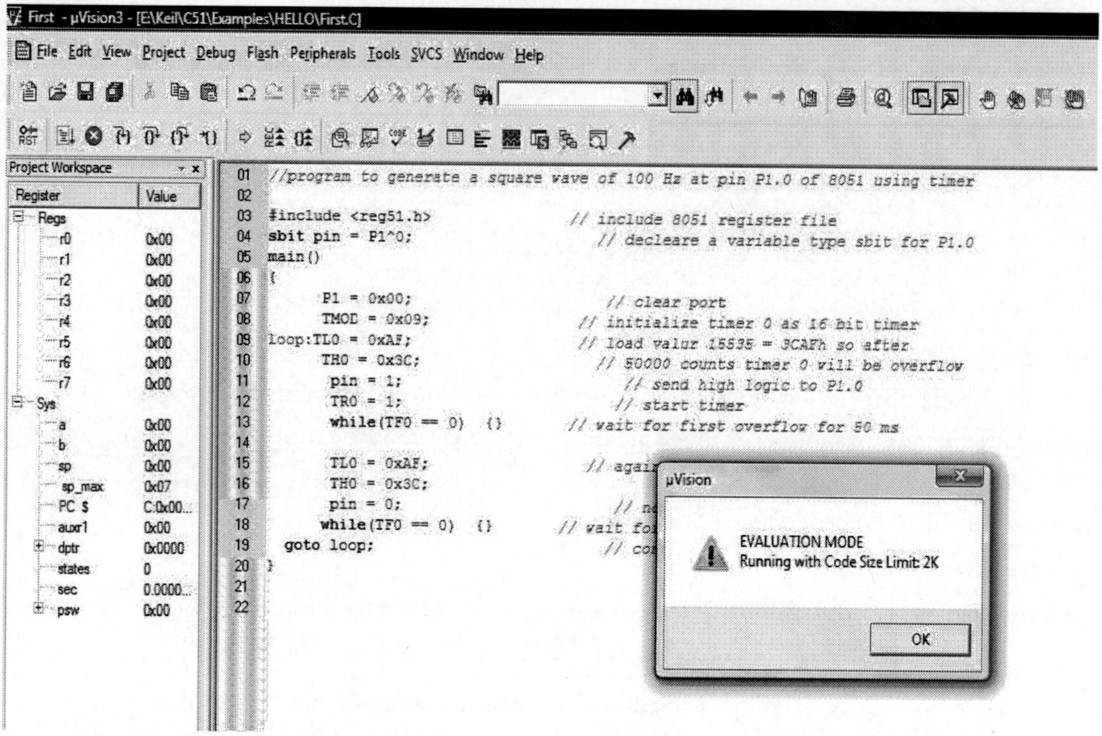

Fig.6.18 Window showing the program running

6.5.5 Creating Hex File

After testing, the program needs to be downloaded on the target board that is 8051. As we have already seen that the controller understands only machine language, so the most important task is to convert the C language program (or assembly language program) to machine language (hex file) Hence, a hex file has to be created to be downloaded on to 8051. Firstly, stop the debug session. The project workspace window will open.

Select project option on toolbar and select "option for target 1" as shown in Fig.6.19.

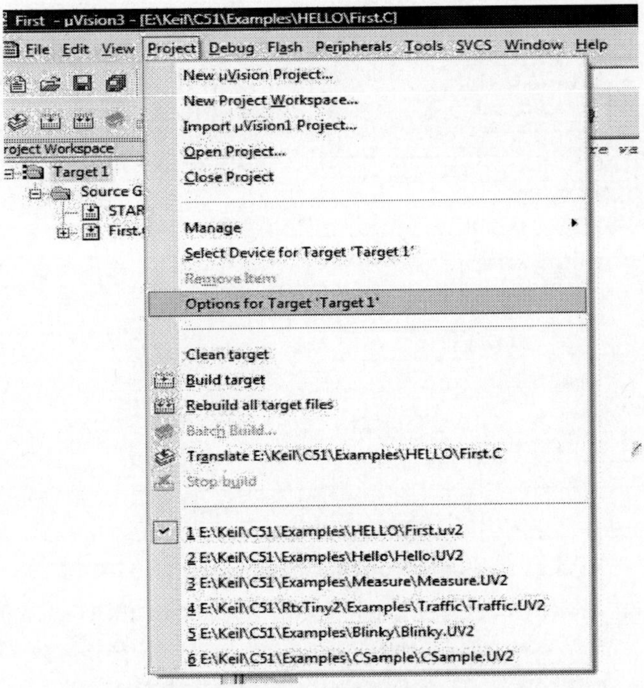

Fig.6.19 Window showing "option for target 1"

On selecting "option for target 1", the window shown in Fig.6.20 will pop up. This window is showing crystal frequency as 33 MHz. But every project needs a different frequency to run. Let us say, in this case, crystal with frequency 11.0592 MHz was used. Accordingly, change the crystal frequency to 11.0592 MHz.

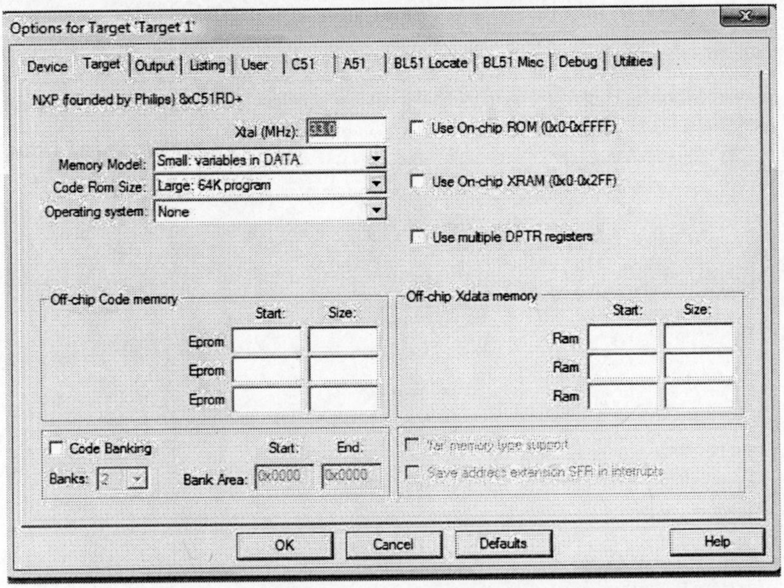

Fig. 6.20 Window showing various options for created project

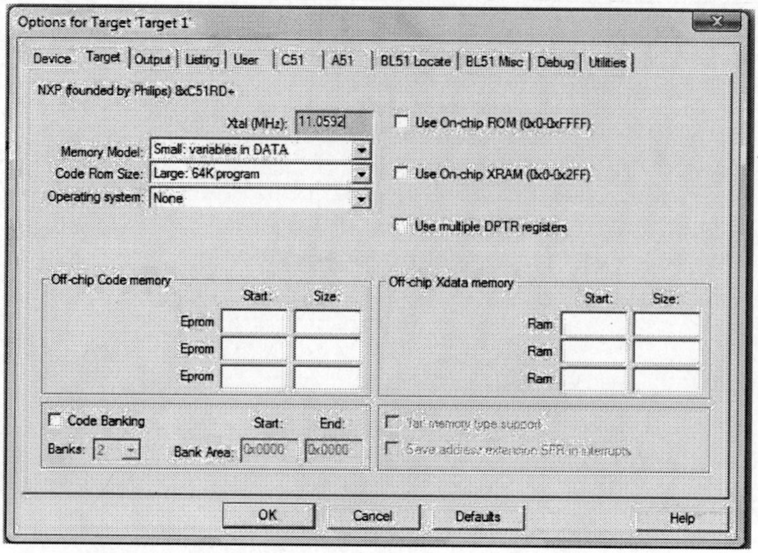

Fig.6.21 Crystal frequency changed to 11.0592 MHz

Now select the output tag shown in Fig.6.22 and mark the "create hex file" box and click ok.

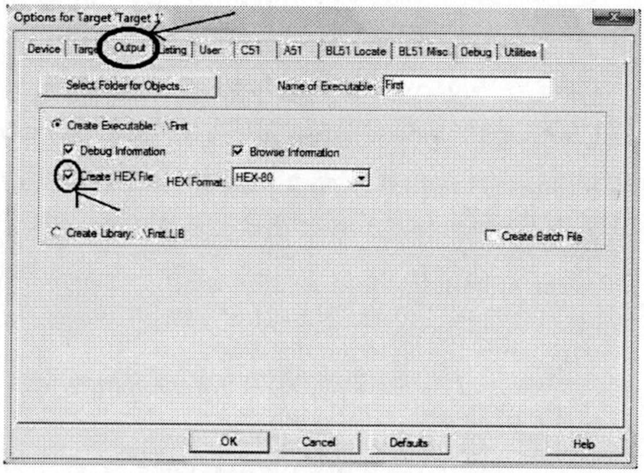

Fig.6.22 Creating Hex file

Now again build the program by clicking on the option "Build target" as shown in Fig.6.23.

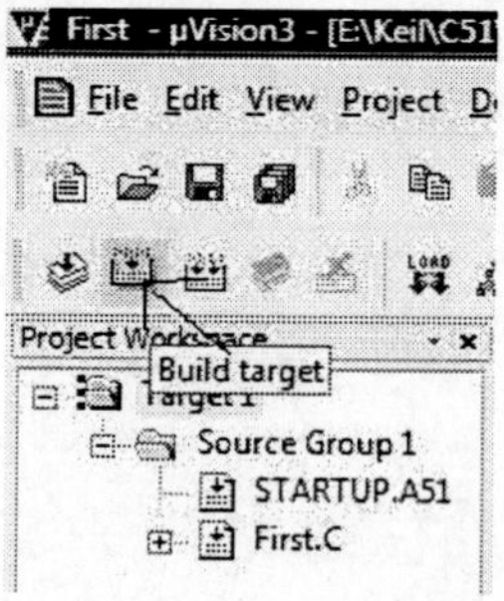

Fig.6.23 Building Target

On building the target, the output window will show the message that a hex file is created as shown in Fig.6.24.

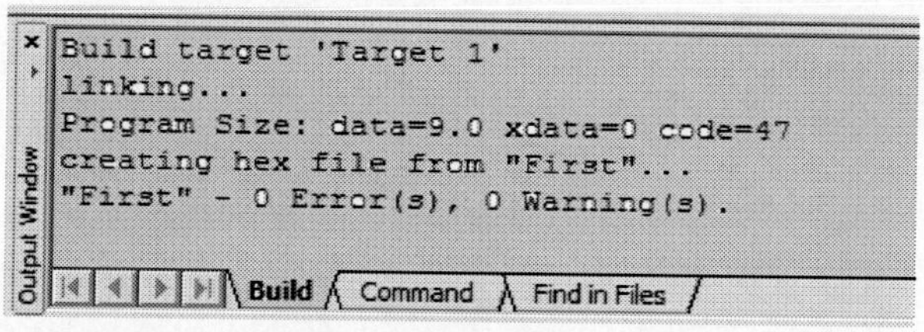

Fig.6.24 Output window showing "hex file is created"

The hex file can also be seen in the project folder with the same name as the project with .hex extension. For example in this case, the hex file created is first.hex as shown in Fig.6.25.

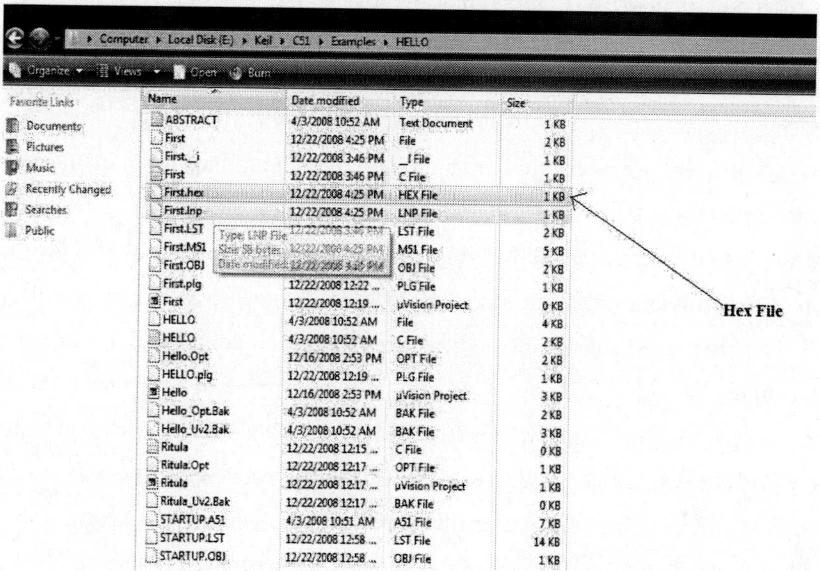

Fig.6.25 Window showing location of created hex file

The hex file can be opened by clicking on first.hex. The notepad window as shown in Fig.6.26 will open up.

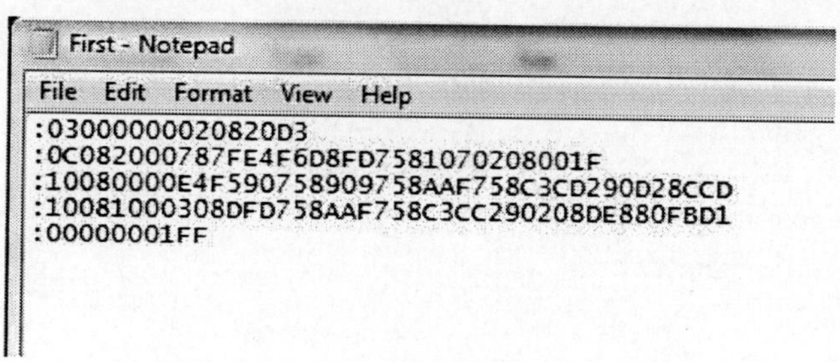

Fig.6.26 Notepad showing Hex File

This file can be directly loaded into the 8051 target board using Flash Magic and the application can be run on the actual environment.

6.6 Burning the Hex file to Program Memory

Following steps should be followed in programming the microcontroller:

(i) Make the required code using KEIL.

(ii) Make the HEX file from the code file.

(iii) Open FLASH MAGIC.

  a) Browse for the location of file.

  b) Click START.

  c) Wait for the message

"FINISHED"

  d) Press reset button on kit make program to run in stand-alone mode.

6.7 FLASH MAGIC

6.7.1 Introduction

A range of microcontrollers are available in market having both on-chip Flash memory and the ability to be reprogrammed using In-System Programming (ISP) technology. Flash Magic is windows software from the Embedded Systems Academy that allows easy access to all the ISP features provided by the devices. It is basically a tool for programming flash based microcontrollers using a serial protocol. It downloads the compiled HEX file to the target microcontroller. Flash Magic provides a clear and simple user interface to these features. It may be noted that Under Windows, only one application may have access the COM Port at any one time, preventing other applications from using the COM Port. Flash Magic only obtains access to the selected COM Port when ISP operations are being performed. This means that other applications that need to use the COM Port, such as debugging tools, may be used while Flash Magic is loaded.

6.7.2 Steps to use Flash-Magic

The various steps to use flash Magic are given below:

(i) Double Click on the icon present on the desktop

(ii) Fig. 6.27 is a screenshot of the main Flash Magic window. The appearance may differ slightly depending on the device selected.

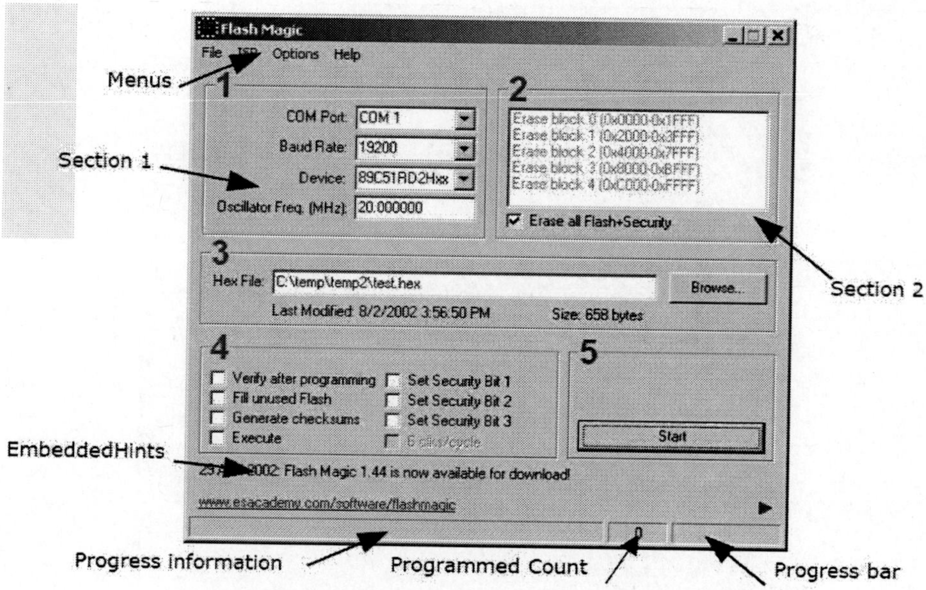

Fig.6.27 Flash Magic Window

The Flash magic window is divided up into five sections. The progress messages will be displayed at the very bottom left of the window and the progress bar is displayed at the very bottom. Embedded Hints, rotating Internet links that can be clicked on to go to a web page using the default browser, are displayed just above the progress information.

(iii) Configuration

On clicking options and advanced options the window shown in Fig.6.28 will be popped.

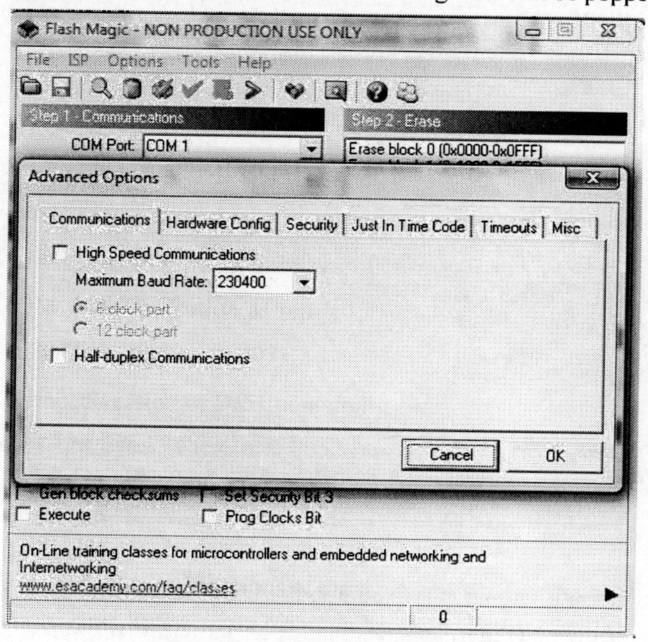

Fig.6.28 Configuration Window

(iv) Click the Hardware Configuration option and set the parameters as shown in Fig.6.29.

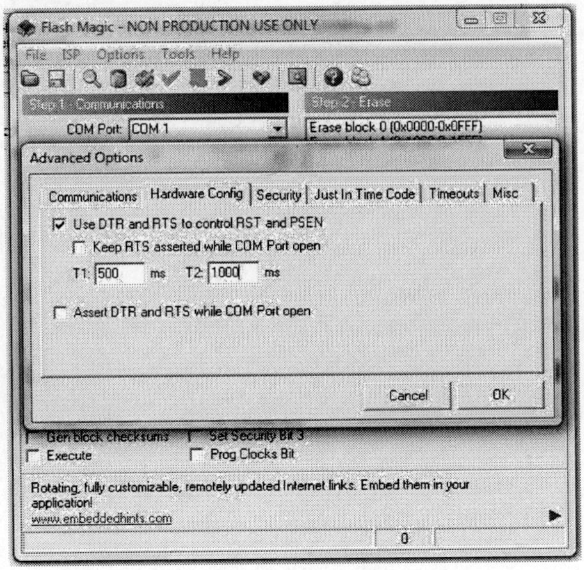

Fig.6.29 Hardware Configuration Window

(v) On clicking ok, the window shown in Fig.6.30 will appear.

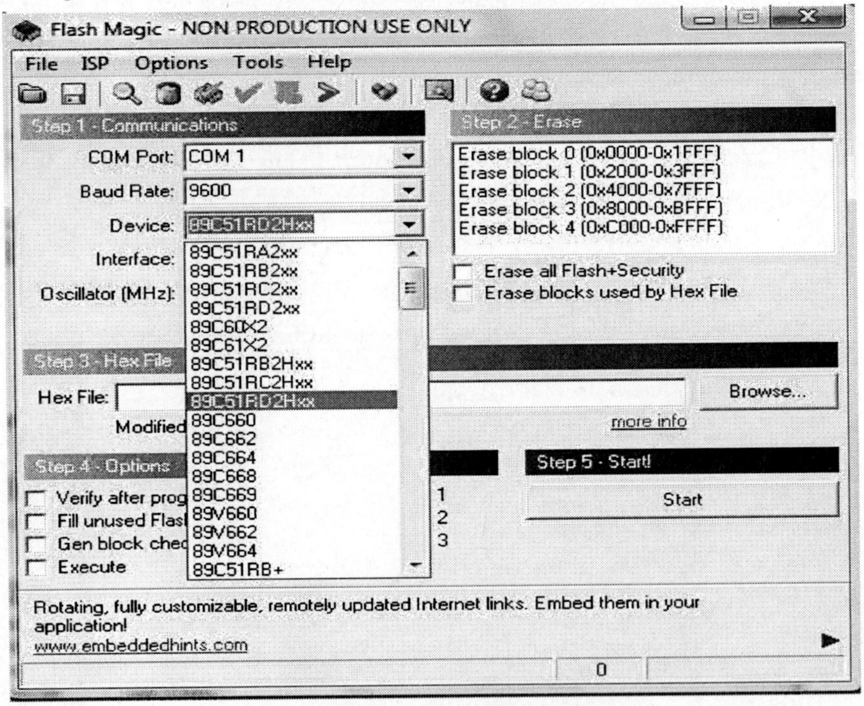

Fig.6.30 Selecting the device

(vi) After selection of the chip (for example, P89C51RD2Hxx in this case), the Com port should be selected as shown in Fig.6.31 depending upon the COM port used for connection. Also set the oscillator frequency as 11.0592 MHz.

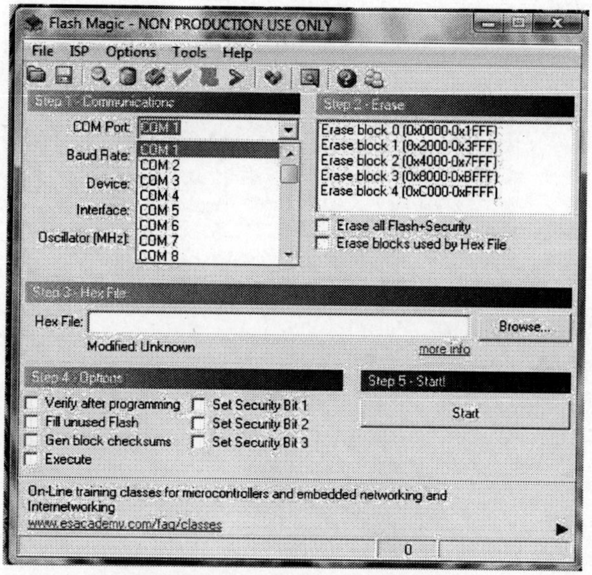

Fig.6.31 Selecting the COM port

(vii) Select the blocks of memory to erase by selecting the section 2 as shown in Fig.6.32.

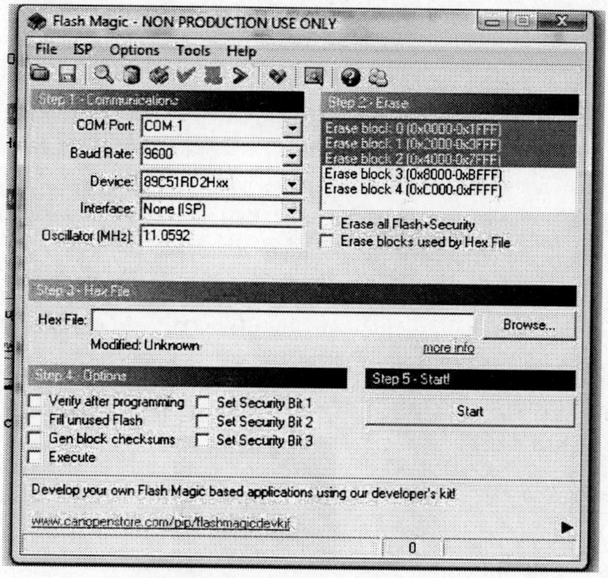

Fig.6.32 Erasing the blocks of memory

(viii) Next step is to browse for the hex file to be loaded. One can either enter a path name in the text box or click on the Browse button to select a Hex File by browsing to it. Also Open… from the File menu can be chosen. The hex file can be loaded as shown in Fig.6.33.

Fig.6.33 Loading the Hex file

(ix) Flash Magic provides various options that may be used after the Hex File has been programmed as shown in Fig.6.34.

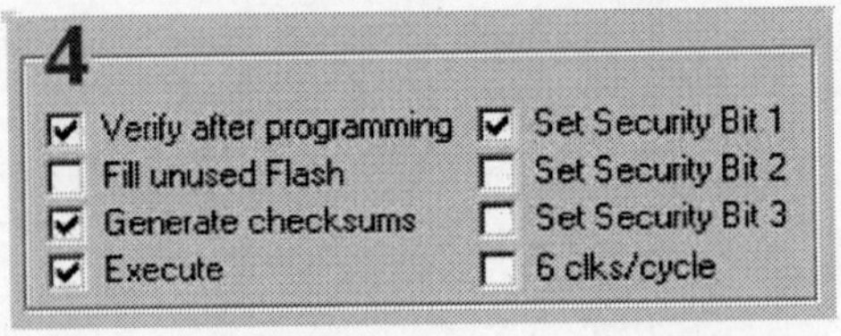

Fig.6.34 Various options in Flash Magic

All these options are described as under:

(a) Verify after programming

If "Verify after Programming" option is checked, it will result in the data contained in the Hex File being read back from Flash and compared with the Hex File after programming. This helps to ensure that the Hex File was correctly programmed.

(b) Fill unused Flash

If "Fill Unused Flash" option is checked, it will result in every memory location not used by the Hex File to be programmed with the value that sets all the bits to a programmed state. Once a location has been programmed with this feature it cannot be reprogrammed with any other value. This will prevent someone from programming the device or altering the application's operation.

(c) Generate checksums

If "Generate Checksums" option is checked, it will instruct Flash Magic to program the highest location in every Flash block used by the Hex File with a special "checksum adjuster value".

(d) Execute

If "Execute" option is checked, it will cause the downloaded firmware to be executed automatically after the programming is complete. It may be noted that this will not work if using the Hardware Reset option or a device that does not support this feature.

(x) After all the features have been set, press the Start button by Clicking the Start button will result in all the selected operations in the main window taking place. Once started, a progress bar and a progress information will be displayed at the bottom of the MAIN window.

(xi) Within 5-6 seconds, the message will be displayed as

"FINISHED".

UNIT SUMMARY

In this chapter on Software Development tools for the 8051 microcontroller, we delved into essential aspects crucial for programming for developing embedded system. We started by exploring various software development tools utilized in development of 8051 programming. Subsequently, we learnt about Keil compilers required for creating Hex file from assembly language and Embedded C programs. Lastly, we examined practical development of project by burning the created hex file into the microcontroller using Flash magic software. Through these discussions, readers gained a comprehensive understanding of how to develop robust and efficient solutions for the 8051 microcontroller.

KNOW MORE

SCAN HERE TO SEE VIDEO ON KEIL COMPILER

EXERCISES

Multiple Choice Questions

6.1 Which software tool is commonly used for programming the 8051 microcontroller?

(a) Keil uVision (b) MPLAB X (c) CodeWarrior (d) AVR Studio

6.2 What type of file is generated by the assembler for the 8051 microcontroller?

(a) .exe (b) .obj (c) .hex (d) .bin

6.3 Which of the following is a popular assembler for 8051 microcontrollers?

(a) MASM (b) TASM (c) NASM (d) A51

6.4 In Keil uVision, which extension is used for source files?

(a) .src (b) .asm (c) .c (d) .8051

6.5 What is the function of a simulator in 8051 development?

(a) Program the microcontroller (b) Simulate the behavior of the microcontroller

(c) Create schematic diagrams (d) Generate machine code

6.6 Which tool is used to upload code to the 8051 microcontroller?

(a) Compiler (b) Linker (c) Loader (d) Debugger

6.7 What does an integrated development environment (IDE) typically include?

(a) Editor, compiler, and debugger (b) Oscilloscope

(c) Logic analyzer (d) Power supply

6.8 Which of the following is a common debugging tool for the 8051?

(a) Logic analyzer (b) In-circuit emulator (ICE)

(c) Function generator (d) Spectrum analyzer

6.9 What is the purpose of the linker in the 8051 development process?

(a) Convert high-level code to assembly code

(b) Assemble source code into object code

(c) Link various object files into a single executable file

(d) Upload code to the microcontroller

6.10 Which programming language is commonly used with the Keil uVision tool for 8051 development?

(a) C++ (b) Java (c) Python (d) C

6.11 What is the function of a cross-compiler in the context of 8051 development?

(a) Compile code for the host computer

(b) Translate high-level code to machine code for the 8051

(c) Debug code on the microcontroller

(d) Simulate the microcontroller's behavior

6.12 Which of the following is NOT a feature of an IDE used for 8051 development?

(a) Code editor (b) Compiler (c) Multimeter (d) Debugger

Answers of Multiple Choice Questions

6.1 (a) , 6.2 (c), 6.3 (d), 6.4 (b), 6.5 (b), 6.6 (c), 6.7 (a), 6.8 (b), 6.9 (c), 6.10 (d), 6.11 (b), 6.12 (c)

Short and Long Answer Type Questions

Short Answer Questions:

6.13 What is the purpose of using Keil uVision in 8051 development?

6.14 Explain the role of an assembler in 8051 microcontroller programming.

6.15 What is the function of a linker in the software development process for 8051 microcontrollers?

6.16 Describe the purpose of a simulator in the context of 8051 microcontroller development.

6.17 Why is a loader used in programming the 8051 microcontroller?

6.18 What components are typically included in an Integrated Development Environment (IDE) for 8051 development?

6.19 How does an in-circuit emulator (ICE) aid in the debugging process for 8051 applications?

6.20 What is a cross-compiler and why is it important for 8051 development?

6.21 Explain the significance of the .hex file in the 8051 development process.

6.22 What advantages does using a high-level language like C offer in 8051 programming compared to assembly language?

6.23 What is the role of a debugger in 8051 software development?

6.24 Why is ROM used for storing program code in the 8051 microcontroller?

6.25 What are the typical steps involved in developing and deploying software for the 8051 microcontroller?

6.26 Describe the function of a project manager tool within an IDE like Keil uVision.

6.27 What is a bootloader and how is it used in 8051 microcontroller programming?

6.28 What types of files are generated during the assembly and linking stages of 8051 development?

6.29 How does the use of a text editor assist in writing assembly language programs for the 8051?

6.30 What is the importance of the ORG directive in 8051 assembly language programming?

6.31 Explain the difference between a simulator and an emulator in the context of 8051 development tools.

REFERENCES

1. Kenneth, Ayala, 8051 Microcontroller Architecture Programming and Application, PHI Learning, New Delhi,ISBN: 978-1401861582
2. Mazidi, Mohmad Ali; Mazidi, Janice Gelispe; MckinlayRoline D., The 8051 Microcontroller and Embedded system, Pearson Education, Delhi, ISBN 978-8177589030
3. Pal, Ajit, Microcontroller Principle and Application, PHI Learning, New Delhi, ISBN 13: 978-81-203-4392-4
4. Deshmukh, Ajay, Microcontroller Theory and Application, McGraw Hill., New Delhi, ISBN-9780070585959
5. Kamal, Raj, Microcontroller Architecture Programming, Interfacing and System Design, Pearson Education India, Delhi, ISBN: 9788131759905
6. Mathur; Panda, Microprocessors and Microcontrollers, PHI Learning, New Delhi, ISBN:978-81-203-5231-5
7. Krishna Kant, Microprocessors and Microcontrollers: Architecture programming and System Design, PHI Learning, New Delhi, ISBN:978-81-203-4853-0
8. www. keil.com

Online Resource References

1. https://onlinecourses.swayam2.ac.in/ntr24_ed63/course
2. https://www.youtube.com/watch?v=_PDxPki0xp8&t=234s
3. https://www.youtube.com/watch?v=M0VljVAfMVE&t=67s
4. https://www.youtube.com/watch?v=BxxLqTtEI9s
5. https://www.youtube.com/watch?v=QfHpXAhXDLo
6. https://www.youtube.com/watch?v=fmCYb5iimm8

CO AND PO ATTAINMENT TABLE

Course outcomes (COs) for this course can be mapped with the programme outcomes (POs) after the completion of the course and a correlation can be made for the attainment of POs to analyze the gap. After proper analysis of the gap in the attainment of POs necessary measures can be taken to overcome the gaps.

Table for CO and PO attainment

Course Outcomes	Expected Mapping with Programme Outcomes *(1- Weak Correlation; 2- Medium correlation; 3- Strong Correlation)*						
	PO-1	PO-2	PO-3	PO-4	PO-5	PO-6	PO-7
CO-1							
CO-2							
CO-3							
CO-4							
CO-5							

The data filled in the above table can be used for gap analysis.

INDEX